# Minutes
# MATTER

10 Commandments
to 2 P. 54

Gods will for es    p.65

# Minutes
# MATTER

MAKING EVERY BEAT COUNT

# K.R. MELE

AMBASSADOR INTERNATIONAL
GREENVILLE, SOUTH CAROLINA & BELFAST, NORTHERN IRELAND
www.ambassador-international.com

# Minutes Matter

Making Every Beat Count

ISBN: 978-1-62020-797-0
eISBN: 978-1-62020-800-7

Cover Photograph Courtesy of Austin Findley
Design & Typesetting by Hannah Nichols
Ebook Conversion by Anna Riebe Raats

AMBASSADOR INTERNATIONAL
Emerald House
411 University Ridge, Suite B14
Greenville, SC 29601, USA
www.ambassador-international.com

AMBASSADOR BOOKS
The Mount
2 Woodstock Link
Belfast, BT6 8DD, Northern Ireland, UK
www.ambassadormedia.co.uk

*The colophon is a trademark of Ambassador, a Christian publishing company.*

*Dedicated in remembrance of Jesus Christ, who taught us how to truly live so that our minutes matter when all is said and done. And to my good friend, Evelyn, who made her minutes matter and impacted many lives around her.*

# Contents

INTRODUCTION                                    9

Chapter 1
HOW MANY?                                       13

Chapter 2
ALL THINGS                                      31

Chapter 3
180 MINUTES A WEEK                              39

Chapter 4
NEXT TO JESUS                                   47

Chapter 5
RIGHT OR LEFT?                                  59

Chapter 6
WHATEVER                                        69

Chapter 7
PAYING IT FORWARD                               81

Chapter 8
TREASURE HUNT                                   89

Chapter 9
WHERE ARE YOU?                                  103

Chapter 10
WHAT IS YOUR LIFE?                              113

CONCLUSION                                      127

ENDNOTES                                        135

# Introduction

*"We manage time, waste time, spend time, and save time. We wish it would come . . . we wish it would pass . . . we see time fly . . . we feel it drag. We watch our clocks and carry calendars . . . yet God controls time."*
—Jon Walker, *God Controls the Timing in Our Lives*[1]

I LOVE HOW THIS IS stated. Yes, we know that we cannot change the amount of time that each day holds and each life is given. But what would our lives look like if we began to view time as something we are called to be managers over, just like our money or resources that God has given us? How differently would we live our passing days if we viewed time as one of the greatest gifts we've been given? This book is not so much a *time management* book as it is a *heart management* book. Many books have been written about how to manage our time. However, I believe time management begins with managing our hearts well. And when we give the proper attention to our hearts, our minutes and moments in life will begin to matter in ways that will make a difference for eternity.

In the only Psalm (90) attributed to Moses, he writes in verse 12, *"So teach us to number our days, That we may gain a heart of wisdom."*

This verse says so much. Just think of this for a moment. Moses wrote about something he wanted to gain that could be accomplished only if he learned how to take account of his days. A heart of wisdom, isn't that something we all yearn for? Unless we learn to number our days, we will never truly gain that heart of wisdom.

Do you remember in the Bible when the Lord God Almighty appeared before Solomon and gave him the opportunity of a lifetime? To ask for whatever he wanted. Let me say that again, whatever he wanted!

Solomon asked for wisdom? Hmm, I don't know about you, but if I had an offer on the table to ask for anything I wanted, I'm not sure wisdom would have been at the top of my list. Can you relate? I mean, there are so many other things that come to my mind before wisdom. But really, it should be. Why? Because if we can gain that type of heart, our days will not be wasted. Let's look at this conversation that Solomon had with God a little closer.

> "Now the king went to Gibeon to sacrifice there, for that was the great high place: Solomon offered a thousand burnt offerings on that altar.
>
> At Gibeon the LORD appeared to Solomon in a dream by night; and God said, "Ask! What shall I give you?"
>
> And Solomon said: "You have shown great mercy to Your servant David my father, because he walked before You in truth, in righteousness, and in uprightness of heart with You; You have continued this great kindness for him, and You have given him a son to sit on his throne, as it is this day.
>
> Now, O LORD my God, You have made Your servant king instead of my father David, but I am a little child; I do not know how to go out or come in.
>
> And Your servant is in the midst of Your people whom You have chosen, a great people, too numerous to be numbered or counted. Therefore give to Your servant an understanding heart to judge Your people, that I may discern between good and evil. For who is able to judge this great people of Yours?"
>
> The speech pleased the Lord, that Solomon had asked this thing.
>
> Then God said to him: "Because you have asked this thing, and have not asked long life for yourself, nor have asked riches for yourself, nor have asked the life of your enemies, but have asked for yourself

*understanding to discern justice, behold, I have done according to your words; see, I have given you a wise and understanding heart, so that there has not been anyone like you before you, nor shall any like you arise after you.*

*And I have also given you what you have not asked: both riches and honor, so that there shall not be anyone like you among the kings all your days.*

*So if you walk in My ways, to keep My statutes and My commandments, as your father David walked, then I will lengthen your days."*
—1 Kings 3:4-14

What a speech! It says that Solomon's *speech pleased the Lord.*

I remember speech class in school, and the closer it got to my turn, the more nervous I became. My speech was before a human being. Could you imagine making a speech before the God of the universe? I wonder how Solomon felt when he woke up from this dream.

Before we move along here, let's ask why Solomon asked for an understanding heart, a heart of wisdom. Did he just desire to be smarter than everyone else? No, it says that he desired it so that he could *discern between good and evil.* The question then becomes, how much do we need that same discerning heart today?

O Lord, give us a heart of wisdom!


Now, to begin this book, let's look at the last part of this text from 1 Kings 3 and couple it with the verse I began with from Psalm 90. I'm going to put them back-to-back to show how these two verses fit like a hand in a glove. Isn't it beautiful how God's Word fits together perfectly from cover to cover?

*"So if you walk in My ways, to keep My statutes and My commandments, as your father David walked, then I will lengthen your days."*
—1 Kings 3:14

*"So teach us to number our days, That we may gain a heart of wisdom."*

—Psalm 90:12

My prayer for this book is that it will cause us to realize that we are given only so many days on this earth and how we use them here will determine much about where and how we will spend eternity. This book is more than another *time management* book; it is a *heart management* book.

There is a verse found in Proverbs that says,

*"Keep your heart with all diligence, For out of it spring the issues of life."*

—Proverbs 4:23

Issues of life? Don't we all have them? But I wonder how many *issues* we have in life because our heart was not kept with all diligence. I believe that as we begin to *number our days, gain a heart of wisdom and learn to walk in His ways*, that our days will be lengthened and used more effectively as we begin to use them for His glory, not just for ourselves.

In the pages to follow, you will find practical ways to *make the most of your days*. I trust that you will be encouraged mostly by the Scriptures I place near the ideas that I share. For without the Word, they are just my opinions and thoughts. I pray that the Word that inspires my thinking will bring light to where you find yourself today.

So enjoy the journey.

Don't waste another minute!

We really don't know how many more we have. So while the clock is still ticking and the heart is still beating, let's get started.

# How Many?

525,600 MINUTES IN A YEAR. 36,792,000 minutes if you are given 70 years and 42,048,000 minutes if you're blessed with 80!

> *"The days of our lives are seventy years; And if by reason of strength they are eighty years, Yet their boast is only labor and sorrow; For it is soon cut off, and we fly away."*
> —Psalm 90:10

Could you imagine at the beginning of our lives if we had the opportunity to check how many minutes we were going to live?

> *26,280,000 – 50 years*
>
> *31,536,000 – 60 years*
>
> *36,792,000 – 70 years*
>
> *42,048,000 – 80 years*

May I ask who wouldn't check the 42,048,000 minute box? I mean, would anyone check less? But when you look at it as minutes, don't all these choices seem like so many?

We must remember, however, the more days we are given, the more we will have to be accountable for over time. We all know this fact to be true, that none of us are guaranteed another minute. So why not strive to make each minute matter and every beat of our heart count? I wholeheartedly believe that as we begin to be good stewards of our days, we will be able to accomplish so much for the Lord because we are honoring Him with one of the most precious gifts we've all been given, time. So where do we begin?

Our days are busy, and without a plan, we will collapse at the end of each day and ask, *"What just hit me?"*

Ever been there?

I'm going to open a window to myself so that you can get a little glimpse of how I'm wired. I've been an organized person for most of my life, at least as long as I can remember. Being disorganized can drive me crazy. I've learned to live by *to-do* lists and when I check something off it makes me feel really good!

I know, kind of weird, huh? But how many of you can relate? Actually, when I do something that wasn't on my list, I'll sometimes write it on my list so that I can receive the pleasure of checking it off my list.

Some of you are laughing and some are relating to this. There are many benefits of being an organized person by your very nature, but the danger of needing organization in your life at every turn is that it can be hard to relax.

That is why the smartest man who ever lived, Solomon, wrote this as well:

> *"Do not be overly righteous, Nor be overly wise: Why should you destroy yourself?*
> *Do not be overly wicked, Nor be foolish: Why should you die before your time?*
> *It is good that you grasp this, And also not remove your hand from the other;*
> *For he who fears God will escape them all."*
> —Ecclesiastes 7:16-18

In another version, it says the man who *"fears God will avoid all extremes"* (NIV).

We must keep a balance in our lives as we use our time wisely in all that we do. We must begin our days asking the Lord to help us in all areas of our lives. In the following chapters, we will look at some practical ways to stay healthy within our personal lives, our families, and our place of work, in worship, in serving and in play. There are various areas of our lives that we will explore to make sure we are making our *minutes matter* in this crazy pace we try and keep called life.

In whatever we do, my prayer is that we make our lives count for something or someone.

The apostle Paul puts it like this when he writes to the Colossian church:

*"And whatever you do, do it heartily, as to the Lord and not to men,*
*knowing that from the Lord you will receive the reward of your*
*inheritance; for you serve the Lord Christ."*
—Colossians 3:23-24

Could Paul have been thinking about what Solomon had in mind when he wrote Ecclesiastes 9:10, *"Whatever your hand finds to do, do it with your might . . . "*?

I'll share more about these thoughts in chapter six called, "Whatever." But for now, no matter how many minutes we're given, let's decide to use them in a wise manner that would be pleasing to our Lord. May we spend them on His plan for our lives, not merely our plans for our lives. When I pray, I sometimes ask the Lord to help me be a good steward of my *time, talent, treasure and thoughts.* I believe that if I get these right, other things will begin to fall into place. I also realize that when I am not being a good steward of these, that I can become self-centered rather than Christ-centered. And I believe it all begins with the condition of our heart.

Jesus puts it this way in Matthew 6:33, *"But seek first the kingdom of God and His righteousness, and all these things shall be added unto you."*

As we seek Christ first and His righteousness in our lives, our numbered days will become days that bring glory to His Name, no matter how many of them we may have left.

## A New Day & A Secret Place

Alarm clocks come in a variety of shapes, sizes, and sounds. Most are on people's phones. These days, I rarely need an alarm clock to wake me up. As you get older, your internal clock begins to wake you up in a variety of ways. I won't go into details, but if you are below forty, enjoy the entire night of sleep without having to get up in the middle of the night, at least once.

That little light on my phone even helped me on a mission trip to Haiti in the middle of the night (or very early in the morning) to find the outside bathroom. I was so thankful for my phone for such a time as this. I did feel bad for the guys sleeping in our outdoor "converted chicken coop," because every time I opened the door it would creak.

Sorry, guys, if you're reading this, I really did try to be quiet.

Before cell phones, I remember when I was a junior in college in 1987. I had a new roommate and the very first night he told me that he set his alarm clock and put it on the other side of the room so that he would have to physically get out of bed to turn it off.

Sounds like a great plan, unless you don't move when your alarm goes off. So the first morning we awoke, well, I awoke, to his alarm going off across the room. He was dead asleep and did not budge. The one thing he did not tell me is that his alarm clock was an old fashioned one that had two bells on the top with a tiny hammer in the middle that would smack those bells back and forth in a fury!

And guess what, it did not have a snooze button, you had to get up and turn it off. Well, when it went off that first morning, I never heard something so loud so early in the morning. I shot out of bed, looked around and thought that a literal locomotive was coming through our bedroom wall.

Oh, it woke me up! But for him, unbelievably, he slept right through it. Let's just say that alarm clock lasted, oh, about a day.

But I truly believe that each new day doesn't start when the alarm clock goes off in the morning. Our today actually begins the night before. As we lie down at night, if we have a plan in mind for the next day, it will cause us to sleep better and wake up ready to go.

Now, I'm not saying you will jump out of bed with wings on your feet.

How many of you are morning people? My wife really doesn't like to talk for about the first hour of the morning. Actually, ever see those shirts, signs, or mugs about coffee?

Here is one I picked up for my wife a few years ago.

When we organize and prepare ourselves for each day the night before, we will then begin to get our days started off on the right beat. Some of these things may seem trivial, but as we discipline ourselves to do them, we will add valuable minutes to the start of every day.

Can anyone relate to getting up too late in the morning, rushing around, trying to figure out what to wear, what to eat, what not to eat, what not to wear, and if you're blessed to be a woman who likes to wear make-up, well, you can add on another chunk of time to your morning. Can I just say right here, I'm glad I'm a guy.

So, how can we get each and every day started off on the right beat? I would assume that if you are a follower of Jesus Christ and desire a close relationship with Him, that you value the importance of spending time with Him every day. But, where do you fit it into your day?

Now, you may not be a morning person, but there are some things that may help carve out some time into your mornings so that you leave your house every day having spent some valuable moments with the One who loves you the most. The One and only One who can cause your heart to beat for all the right reasons.

*"Give ear to my words, O LORD,*

*Consider my meditation.*

*Give heed to the voice of my cry,*

*My King and my God,*

*For to you I will pray.*

*My voice You shall hear in the morning, O LORD;*

*In the morning I will direct it to You,*

*And I will look up."*

—Psalm 5:1-3

David writes here of a special time *in the morning* that he would meditate, cry out, and look up to God in prayer. Then he says, *"My voice You shall hear in the morning, O LORD."*

Now, this doesn't mean that God hears our voice only in the mornings when we pray. He listens for our voice anytime we cry out to Him. Whether it be at the break of dawn, throughout our day, in the evening, or in the middle of the night. But there is something about the first part of the day being set apart for Him that I believe not only blesses Him, but gets our heart beating in the right direction for the day that is about to unfold before us. When we begin our day with prayer, it helps set that pattern in our hearts for the rest of the day of *praying without ceasing* that Paul speaks of in 1 Thessalonians 5:17.

In another Psalm we read, *"But to You I have cried out, O LORD, And in the morning my prayer comes before You"* (88:13).

Yes, God can hear our prayers in the afternoon, the evening, or late at night. Actually, prayer is to be a continual activity that is constant throughout every minute of our day. As we just read above, the Apostle Paul reminds us to *pray without ceasing.*

And a time that is set apart with the Lord before we head out the door each morning is vital to our ongoing relationship that Jesus wants to have with us as we walk throughout our days. I believe the prayers we have to quickly *cry out* to Him at two in the afternoon are more effective and powerful when they are built upon a consistent prayer time that begins our days.

To pray without ceasing, we must be praying in the first place. We must not ignore that prayer time in the mornings and only *call upon Him* in the busyness of our days. But as we *seek Him first,* then in the midst of our days, His ear will be very inclined to hear us when we call.

Do you ever have moments throughout your day that you just *shoot up a prayer* to the Lord? Why is it when we get in the midst of our days we can easily forget to pray and just try to figure out things on our own?

I believe one of the greatest examples of offering up a quick prayer to the Lord and having it answered is found in the book of Nehemiah.

> *"And it came to pass in the month of Nisan, in the twentieth year of King Artaxerxes, when wine was before him, that I took the wine and gave it to the king. Now I had never been sad in his presence before.*
>
> *Therefore the king said to me, "Why is your face sad, since you are not sick? This is nothing but sorrow of heart." So, I became dreadfully afraid,*
>
> *and said to the king, "May the king live forever! Why should my face not be sad, when the city, the place of my fathers' tombs, lies waste, and its gates are burned with fire?"*
>
> *Then the king said to me, "What do you request?" So I prayed to the God of heaven.*
>
> *And I said to the king, "If it pleases the king, and if your servant has found favor in your sight, I ask that you send me to Judah, to the city of my fathers' tombs, that I may rebuild it."*
>
> *Then the king said to me (the queen also sitting beside him), "How long will your journey be? And when will you return?" So it pleased the king to send me; and I set him a time."*
>
> —Nehemiah 2:1-6

This story encourages my heart so much because it reminds me how God is always ready to not only hear our prayers, but also answer them when we call. But there is something key that transpired before this conversation between Nehemiah and the king took place. It was a conversation between Nehemiah and the real King.

You see, when the earthly king asked Nehemiah the question, *"What do you request?"* Nehemiah didn't have time to say, *"Hold on, I have to go pray for an hour before I answer you, I'll be right back."* No, it says right at that moment, *"So I prayed to the God of heaven. And I said to the king."*

Nehemiah's first response when asked this question was to do what? Pray . . . and then he gives his answer.

No delay, no thinking about what to say. Nehemiah simply *prayed and answered.*

But why was he so confident in doing so? Why was he so inclined to pray in a heartbeat? Well, let's rewind to the verses in chapter one of Nehemiah before this conversation ever took place with the king.

> *"It came to pass in the month of Chislev, in the twentieth year, as I was in Shushan the citadel,*
>
> *that Hanani one of my brethren came with men from Judah; and I asked them concerning the Jews who had escaped, who had survived the captivity, and concerning Jerusalem.*
>
> *And they said to me, 'The survivors who are left from the captivity in the province are there in great distress and reproach. The wall of Jerusalem is also broken down, and its gates are burned with fire.'*
>
> *So it was, when I heard these words, that I sat down and wept, and mourned for many days; I was fasting and praying before the God of heaven.*
>
> *And I said: 'I pray, LORD God of heaven, O great and awesome God, You who keep your covenant and mercy with those who love You and observe Your commandments,*

*please let Your ear be attentive and Your eyes open, that You may hear the prayer of Your servant which I pray before You now, day and night, for the children of Israel Your servants, and confess the sins of the children of Israel which we have sinned against You. Both my father's house and I have sinned.*

*We have acted very corruptly against You, and have not kept the commandments, the statutes, nor the ordinances which You commanded Your servant Moses.*

*Remember, I pray, the word that You commanded Your servant Moses, saying, "If you are unfaithful, I will scatter you among the nations;*

*but if you return to Me, keep My commandments and do them, though some of you were cast out to the farthest part of the heavens, yet I will gather them from there, and bring them to the place which I have chosen as a dwelling for My name."*

*Now these are Your servants and Your people, whom You have redeemed by Your great power, and by Your strong hand.*

*O Lord, I pray, please let Your ear be attentive to the prayer of Your servant, and to the prayer of Your servants who desire to fear Your name; and let Your servant prosper this day, I pray, and grant him mercy in the sight of this man.' For I was the king's cupbearer."*
—Nehemiah 1:1b-11

Now we begin to understand the reason that Nehemiah was so quick to call out to God immediately when the king asked him a question. I could see Nehemiah in those few seconds taking a breath and praying, *"God, help me with my answer."*

The interesting fact here is the amount of time that Nehemiah spent praying before he went to the king. If you look at this story closely, you will see that from the time that Nehemiah heard the report concerning Jerusalem *(month of Chislev—our November/December)* to the moment he went to the king *(month of Nisan—our March/April)* was four months. For these four months, Nehemiah spent time in prayer and fasting.

Remember in verse four it says, *"For some days I mourned and fasted."* Nehemiah was serious about learning how to *pray without ceasing.* It seems as you read the book of Nehemiah that he was always calling out to God at the drop of a hat. Many times you will find him going about his day and at the same time, praying. Nehemiah simply had a personal relationship with God because he established times of prayer and fasting which then transformed his days into times of communication with God throughout his days.

That's what prayer is, talking with God. The more we establish that time with the Lord in our *prayer closets,* the more we will communicate with Him when we are outside those *closets.*

Even Jesus demonstrated the secret of times of prayer with His Father that would then propel Him into His days:

*"Now in the morning, having risen a long while before daylight, He went out and departed to a solitary place; and there He prayed."*

—Mark 1:35

*"Now it came to pass in those days that He went out to the mountain to pray, and continued all night in prayer to God. And when it was day, He called His disciples to Himself."*

—Luke 6:12-13a

Again, we know the Lord can speak to us all times of the day, and He does. But I believe that if we spend time with Him in the mornings, that it causes our ears to be more attuned to His voice.

Why mornings? Mornings are usually quiet. I believe it's easier to *"be still and know that He is God"* (Psalm 46:10) in the mornings. But whether it's mornings or evenings, the importance in learning how to *pray without ceasing* throughout our days is to develop times of extended prayer with our Heavenly Father.

With how hectic things can get, the question becomes, "How can we develop this set time of prayer in our lives?"

A key to establishing this discipline is to have a plan in mind of what your day is going to consist of before you sit down for your time with the Lord. Take time before going to bed each night to review what the next day is going to look like. Pretty soon, after you do this for a period of time, it will become a natural discipline in your life that you won't be able to live without.

Remember, the goal each day is to find a consistent, regular time to get alone with the Lord. No phones, no distractions, no Facebook checking, no animals . . . just you and the Lord. And even though it can be very quiet in the morning, it's amazing how noisy it can be inside of us. We must learn to discipline and quiet our hearts so that we can begin to hear His voice more clearly. And that simply takes, well, time.

I mention animals because the minute my eyes open our cat, Ping, is meowing wanting to be fed, and then usually follows me into where I spend my quiet time with the Lord. Funny thing is that she loves my small cookies that I have with my coffee and I usually give in to her as she enjoys a few small pieces with me. She can be very annoying.

Then, when our dog, Chester, wakes up, he needs to go to the bathroom, and then sometimes will find his way into "my space" as well. Here is a photo of one of my "quiet times" with the Lord . . . and Ping and Chester!

Ping and Chester

What I'm trying to say cannot be understated. Without a quiet, disciplined time with the Lord to start our day, our hearts will never begin on the right beat.

We must find a secret place to escape and simply be with Jesus. A place that is holy and set apart for time with your very best friend. No one loves us like Jesus, and He desires to hang out with us!

Sometimes I get a picture in my mind of Jesus watching us run around in the morning as we strive to get our day started. All the while, He is sitting by watching us frantically do the things to get out the door and hope that all the kids have the correct two shoes on, or shoes at all. I see Jesus simply watching us, shaking His head and saying, *"Would you just come sit with me for a few minutes and let me start your day the right way?"*

If we are to make every minute of our day matter, we must get our hearts beating on the right beat as we start our days. Then, as we structure our days around the *heartbeat of our Lord and Savior,* we will then make every minute count and our activities throughout the day will bring glory to God, no matter what may try and come against us that day.

What is it with a secret place? Well, whether you realize it or not, you were made in a secret place, and our Lord still desires to meet with you in a secret place. Look at what David said when he wrote about this in Psalm 139:

> *"For You formed my inward parts; You covered me in my mother's womb.*
>
> *I will praise You, for I am fearfully and wonderfully made; Marvelous are Your works, And that my soul knows very well.*
>
> *My frame was not hidden from You, When I was made in secret, And skillfully wrought in the lowest parts of the earth.*
>
> *Your eyes saw my substance, being yet unformed. And in Your book they all were written,*
>
> *The days fashioned for me, When as yet there were none of them."*
>
> —Psalm 139:13-16

Wow! I'm no theologian, and I believe that even the greatest minds out there cannot even fathom or explain the depths of these verses. Look at this line one more time:

> *"... when I was made in secret ... "*

There is something about a secret place.

Did you have one as a child? A secret hideout, a treehouse, a place you escaped to be alone? To dream, to just get away and think, rest, relax, or maybe even cry? In these secret places things are quiet.

Even when someone tells a secret, what do they do? They whisper. God wants to meet with you again in a *secret place*. Not where all the noise and commotion is, not where there is confusion and voices clamoring for your attention. It's His still small voice that we need to hear the most. And unfortunately it is the one that can get drowned out very quickly in the noise of our days.

Even in our times of trouble, the Lord invites us into a secret place. Sometimes it can be quite frightening to be completely still and quiet before the Lord God Almighty for too long.

But look what David also writes about this secret place in Psalm 27:5:

> *"For in the time of trouble*
> *He shall hide me in His pavilion;*
> *In the secret place of His tabernacle*
> *He shall hide me;*
> *He shall set me high upon a rock."*

Take a look at a few other places the word "secret" is used in this same context:

> *"He who dwells in the secret place of the Most High*
> *Shall abide under the shadow of the Almighty."*
> —Psalm 91:1

> *"You called in trouble, and I delivered you;*
> *I answered you in the secret place of thunder;*
> *I tested you at the waters of Meribah."*
> —Psalm 81:7

When my kids were growing and beginning to go through challenging seasons in life, I would often direct them to the Psalms because of the very raw and very real writings of the Psalmists.

Aren't you glad for the book of Psalms? Maybe you are in a season in your life that you need to begin with Psalm 1 and continue to Psalm 150. Take your time, let the anointed words of each writer comfort, heal, and soothe your soul as you read. There is healing that comes through the Word in that secret place.

Do you remember the story when the prophet Elijah had a great victory on Mount Carmel, but then found himself in deep depression as Jezebel sent messengers after him to hunt him down?

Elijah finds himself under a broom tree and in 1 Kings 19:4b it says:

> "And he prayed that he might die, and said, 'It is enough! Now, LORD, take my life, for I am no better than my fathers!'"

Shortly after this, he then finds himself running for his life and ends up in a cave, hiding. The Lord calls to him and says, *"Go out, and stand on the mountain before the LORD"* (1 Kings 19:11a).

Here is what happens next:

> "And behold, the LORD passed by, and a great and strong wind tore into the mountains and broke the rocks in pieces before the LORD, but the LORD was not in the wind; And after the wind an earthquake, but the LORD was not in the earthquake;
>
> and after the earthquake a fire; but the LORD was not in the fire; and after the fire a still small voice."
>
> —1 Kings 19:11b-12

Did you notice *the Lord was not in the wind, not in the earthquake and not in the fire?* But when the still small voice spoke, Elijah heard the Lord. Read on . . .

> "So it was, when Elijah heard it, that he wrapped his face in his mantle and went out and stood in the entrance of the cave. Suddenly a voice came to him, and said, 'What are you doing here, Elijah?'"
>
> —1 Kings 19:13

You see, Elijah heard and responded to God's *still small voice.*

We must do the same because the days are full of fire, earthquakes, and wind that will make us want to quit. The key to peaceful living is to learn how to truly be still and know that He is God *(Psalm 46:10)*.

I heard a great quote from Chuck Swindoll as I was listening to one of his radio shows one morning. He said, *"God never reveals His truth to a hurried soul."*[2]

Oh, so true.

My *secret places* at home are one of two. When the weather is nice, it is on my front porch. In colder months, I have a place in my office and a special place where I sit. It's a place that has become very special to me. The chair that I use in my office was my Granpap Joe's. I love this chair. He was a quiet man and a very deep thinker. This is where I learn to *be still and know that He is God* before my day gets rolling.

Whenever I go on a trip, one of the things I scope out is a "secret place." When I was on a mission trip in Haiti in 2015, I found a *secret place* on a rooftop and watched the sunrise early in the morning. Someone had told me about this spot and I could not wait to experience on my own each morning as the sun was rising. These places are very special to me.

Find your *secret place* and allow the Lord to show and speak to you His love, His plan, and His purposes over your life.

Here are some practical tips for starting every day on the right beat:

- Get to bed earlier than you do right now. Make a goal to fall asleep one hour earlier over the next month. Remember, tomorrow starts the day before. At night, turn off the television by a certain time and step away from social media.

- This may sound strange, but pick out your clothes that you are going to wear the night before. Believe it or not, this will save you five, ten, even fifteen minutes every morning. How many of you ever changed your mind several times in the morning because you can't decide what to wear? Waste that time the night before when you're tired, not in the morning.

- Make and pack your lunch (and kids lunches) the night before. If your kids are young, begin to help them the night before to pick out their clothes and help pack the lunches for the next day.
- Sometimes I will even go as far as setting the coffee cups out the night before. If you're married, guys, it's a wise thing to also do the same for your wife while you're at it.

The more disciplined we become the night before, the more time we give ourselves to spend with Jesus and His Word in the morning. Everything I mentioned above will add anywhere from an hour to one and half hours to your morning. Now the key is to not add anything else to this saved time in the morning except your time with the Lord. And by all means, don't forget to set your alarm to wake you up an hour earlier. And do not hit that snooze button!

Okay, maybe once on a cold winter morning.

Jesus wants to wake us up to a new beginning each new day, and as we honor Him with the first part of our day, I guarantee you that you'll begin to see your days in a whole new light. It may take a cup of coffee or so to get moving, but may we begin each new day looking at it from His perspective, and that comes only by spending time in His Word in that secret place.

How many *new days* might you and I have ahead of us? Well, none of us really know. But may we join with Moses in praying, *"Teach us to number our days, That we may gain a heart of wisdom."*

## CHAPTER 1 - SMALL GROUP DISCUSSION

Do you look at time as a gift? If so, how would you say you are spending your minutes? Are there many wasted minutes used up in your day on meaningless things?

Are you enjoying life with a purpose or simply "getting through another day?"

How do you begin your mornings? Do you start your today with a plan in mind the night before? What are some things you can begin to do the night before to add more minutes with the Lord to your mornings?

Have you made a regular time with the Lord a priority in your life? If not, what can you do to carve out some time with Him during your day?

"To pray without ceasing, we must be praying in the first place." How would you say your prayer life is right now in your life?

Practical Application: During this next week, log your minutes on how you spend your time.

**Read Nehemiah 2:1-6**.

- How inclined am I to stop and pray in the midst of my day?
- Why was Nehemiah so ready to pray and answer the king? (See Nehemiah 1)

Ask yourself, "How can I develop a set time of prayer in my life?"

Where could your "secret place" be that you meet with the Lord daily?

# All Things

*For bodily exercise profits a little, but godliness is profitable for all things,*
*having promise of the life that now is and of that which is to come.*
*This is a faithful saying and worthy of all acceptance.*
—1 Timothy 4:8-9

I HAVE A GOOD FRIEND who does not care much for *bodily exercise*. He says that our hearts have only so many beats over a lifetime and if we make them beat faster, well, we will use them up a whole lot quicker. I hope you are laughing right now and not agreeing with him. Actually, the other day he told me that he exercised to start his day and I asked him, *"Doing what?"* and he said, *"I walked down the stairs."*

I'll talk more about the importance of keeping our bodies in good physical shape in the next chapter, but for now, let's talk about the most important thing that we can work on, which Paul tells Timothy is *godliness*. And if we faithfully build this into our lives, the promise God offers us is awesome!

Have you ever had someone break a promise that they made to you? Who hasn't? Sometimes the most difficult thing to handle is when someone makes a promise or gives you their word, and then you never hear from them again or they never follow through. Whether it's a *little promise* or a *big promise*, a promise is a promise and our words should mean something. The great thing about God's Word is that you can count on it! There are 783,137 words in the King James Version of the Bible, and every one of them is reliable and true.

Every single one of them. If you would take time and type the Bible at a pace of sixty words per minute, you would have very sore fingers since it would take about 217.5 hours to retype the entire Bible. That's nine straight days to type 3,116,480 letter characters (www.wordcounter.net).

The Bible has sixty-six books. Thirty-nine are in the Old Testament and twenty-seven in the New Testament, and not until the 12th century were they divided into chapters. The longest chapter is Psalm 119 and the shortest, Psalm 117. Once it was divided, the total number of chapters became 1,189, but it was still rather hard to find your way around. So, in the 16th century the idea was born to number the verses as well. Of the 31,102 verses, the shortest one is: John 11:35, "Jesus wept," and the longest is found in Esther 8:9 with seventy-eight words.

> "So the king's scribes were called at that time, in the third month, which is the month of Sivan, on the twenty-third day; and it is written, according to all that Mordecai commanded, to the Jews, the satraps, the governors, and the princes of the provinces from India to Ethiopia, one hundred and twenty-seven provinces in all, to every province in its own script, to every people in their own language, and to the Jews in their own script and language."

We also know that there are ten commandments and Jesus wrapped them all up with the two greatest commandments:

> "Jesus answered him, "The first of all the commandments is: 'Hear, O Israel, the LORD our God, the LORD is one.
> And you shall love the LORD your God with all your heart, with all your soul, with all your mind, and with all your strength.' This is the first commandment.
> And the second, like it, is this: 'You shall love your neighbor as yourself.' There is no other commandment greater than these."
> —Mark 12:29-31

But if you were to count up the commands in the Bible, you would tally up 6,468. There are also 8,000 predictions, and get this, 1,260 promises.

One thousand two hundred and sixty promises and every single one of them are infallible and inerrant! Let's look at the one promise that I began this chapter with from 1 Timothy 4:8.

*". . . godliness is profitable for all things, having promise of the life that now is and of that which is to come."*

Note that *godliness* is profitable for how many things? Everything and anything imaginable. You name it, you will profit from God's Word as you develop godliness in your life. Have questions about relationships? It's in there!

How about heaven? It's in there! Money, finances . . . yep, in there! Pride, gossip, how the world began, in there! Marriage, how to treat your wife or husband, how to communicate, and yes, even sex . . . it's in there!

Do you remember the commercial years ago about a spaghetti sauce named Prego? To set it up, a father comes into the kitchen where his son and new wife are and there is a pot of sauce on the stove with a jar of Prego beside it.

The father says, "What's this, married six months and your wife is already using spaghetti sauce from a jar?"

The son says, "Pop, this is Prego."

The dad says, "Listen to me, the ingredients of a successful marriage . . . garlic, little bits of herbs and onions for that homemade taste . . ."

The son says, "Look, it's in there," and he puts a spoon with some sauce on it into his dad's mouth.

The father tastes it and says, "It's in there."

For a time, I taped a handmade note on the inside cover of one of my Bibles that said, *"It's in there!"* I could go on and on because everything we ever have a question about is found in God's Word. And when we begin to train our lives to live by it, we will find the answer to the problems we've been searching for all our lives.

In the year 1984, I graduated from Springdale High School. Springdale is a small community about twenty miles or so north of the city of Pittsburgh, Pa. I did not accept Jesus Christ as my Lord and Savior until 1988 when I was twenty-one years old. In our graduation yearbook, they made you come up with a quote that they would place under your picture and name. I remember thinking, *"What in the world am I going to write?"*

When I wrote this below my picture at eighteen years old, I had no idea what I was talking about. I was just trying to come up with something creative. Guess what, now I know exactly what I was talking about.

Kenneth Raymond Mele
Life is nothing but one big problem, but once you solve it, you never forget it.

You see, life really is nothing but one big problem, but once you solve it (Jesus), you never forget it! He doesn't take all your problems away, but He gives you the strength to overcome them. He helps you in the difficult times of life which we all have. Maybe you have heard someone quote this very popular statement before: *God won't give you more than you can handle.* Many people believe this is in the Bible. It was even in one commentary I read in a Study Bible, they had this very quote in the notes. I've even heard a preacher use this quote in a message and state, *"God's Word says . . . "*

But guess what, it isn't in the Bible, and neither do I believe it. Let me explain. First of all, God will always give us more than we can handle, because if we could handle it, we wouldn't need Him. Now there is a verse I believe that this saying gets confused with that says:

*"No temptation has overtaken you except such as is common to man; but God is faithful, who will not allow you to be tempted beyond what you are able, but with the temptation will also make the way of escape, that you may be able to bear it."*
—1 Corinthians 10:13

Yes, it's true, God will not allow us to be *tempted* beyond what we can handle, but will make an escape for us. But when it comes to life in general, I need His help every day because it is much more than I could ever handle on my own.

This I do know, *"For when I am weak, then I am strong"* (2 Corinthians 12:10b).

So the question each one of us must answer if we are going to make every beat and every minute matter is, *"How am I training myself in the Word?"*

Is it a vital part of our existence that we cannot live without? Think of it as water and bread. They say that we could live without water for three days. One reason is that about sixty percent of our body is made up of it and needs water to keep functioning properly. Without it, we would die. Same with food. Now, we can go quite a bit longer without food, depending upon a number of factors. But we all know that eventually we would die by denying our bodies both of these.

How about air? About three minutes.


There is a song written by Michael W. Smith called *Breathe.*[3] Check out a few of the lyrics:

*This is the air I breathe*
*This is my daily bread*
*Your very word spoken to me*

Sometimes I will have someone say to me, *"I just want God to speak to me."*

And at that moment, if I had a Bible in my hands, I would hand it to them and say, *"He already has."*

You see, every word and all 1,260 promises that are in there are just for you. The question becomes *do we have time to discover them?* We must if we are going to train ourselves in godliness.

So let's ask ourselves, "Is His Word really my daily bread or am I eating from a different table? Is His presence the very air I breathe? Do our spirits need Jesus and His Word more than the food we eat, the water we drink, and the air we breathe?"

I love the thought we find in John 1:1-2 that says:

> *"In the beginning was the Word, and the Word was with God, and the Word was God.*
> *He was in the beginning with God."*

This tells us that the Word (Jesus) was with God in the very beginning of time. Actually the verse following this tells us *all things were made through Him, and without Him nothing was made that was made.*

Simply amazing that Jesus, who was with God in the beginning and without Him nothing would have been made, wants to hang out and have a personal relationship with us! And do you know how He does it? By us spending time with Him, His Word.

And remember, training yourself with His Word is profitable for how many things? All things.

The promise that Paul reminded young Timothy of was that it would benefit him both *now* and also for the *life to come* beyond the grave. Now that is what I call making every minute count!

Is there any greater thing that we can do to train ourselves in godliness than to spend time in God's Word? I will make you this promise, you will never regret one minute you spend in God's Word. Don't ever forget, *it's in there!* Every ingredient you need to live a life that glorifies God is in His Word, so dig in. If we get this right and prioritize His Word and His Presence in our lives, the rest will fall into place because of our obedience. Jesus put it this way:

*"But seek first the kingdom of God and His righteousness, and all these things shall be added to you."*
—Matthew 6:33

The Apostle Paul learned the importance of developing godliness and passed it along to Timothy . . . and to us. His Word is waiting to take root in our hearts and become our very first priority. When that happens, things will begin to change all around and especially within us. May it truly become the air we breathe every minute of every day. Let's not let another day go by without making His Word and His Presence our top priority.

## CHAPTER 2 - SMALL GROUP DISCUSSION

**Read 1 Timothy 4:8.** What are some of the *all things* that you have seen God do in your life as you have been growing in Christ?

Do you find it true that God gives you *more than you can handle* because He wants you to depend on Him for the strength you need to overcome?

How would you say that you are doing at training yourself in the Word of God? If this is a struggle, what can you do differently to make this a priority in your life?

**Matthew 6:33** tells us to *"seek first the kingdom of God and His righteousness and all these things shall be added unto you."*

- What would you say it looks like to seek first the kingdom and His righteousness?
- What does Jesus mean when He says, *"all these things shall be added unto you"*?

# 180 Minutes A Week

THERE ARE A LOT OF things we do with our time, right? Think about it.

First let's start with children. Boy, do they love to sleep! Go to school, not so much.

According to the National Sleep Foundation, *babies, children and teens need significantly more sleep than adults to support their rapid mental and physical development.*[4] I found these numbers, well, exhilarating! Maybe you will as well.

| Age | Recommended Amount of Sleep |
|---|---|
| 0-3 months | 14-17 hours (oh, to be an infant again!) |
| 4-11 months | 12-15 hours |
| 1-2 years | 11-14 hours |
| 3-5 years | 10-13 hours |
| 6-13 years | 9-11 hours |
| 14-17 years | 8-10 hours |
| 18-25 years | 7-9 hours |

These are the amounts that most children need to be fully rested. (sleepfoundation.org – *"How much sleep do babies and kids need?"*)

Most adults require between seven and a half to nine hours per night. But take a look at what else we do with our time according to an article from the *Wall Street Journal*—"How Americans Spend Their Time."[5]

- In 2015, Americans slept an average of eight hours and fifty minutes a day, thirteen minutes more than a decade earlier and two minutes more than in 2014.
- Leisure time—five hours and thirteen minutes a day is spent on activities including watching television, socializing, and exercise.
- On weekdays, Americans with full-time jobs spent eight hours and eight minutes a day working or travelling to work, five minutes more than a decade earlier.
- Women spent two hours and fourteen minutes on household activities last year, while men only spent one hour and twenty-six minutes on the same chores.
- Men spend forty-three minutes more a day on leisure activities, including watching TV. Women sleep slightly more—about twenty-five extra minutes per day.

Why am I sharing all these numbers? Let's bring it close to our home and think about how much time we spend on certain activities. Sleep, work, family time, worship, social media, exercise. There is a host of things that can eat up our minutes on any given day. If not careful, the time we spend on meaningless things can become staggering!

Let me share a personal example.

Growing up in Pittsburgh, my favorite sport was baseball and my team . . . the Pittsburgh Pirates! By the way, on a side note, my daughter and I just went to a Pirates game a few weeks ago and I caught my first foul ball . . . with one hand. It surprised me as well! Having gone to games for forty years and never catching a foul ball, I must say, it was pretty exciting. My daughter couldn't believe it either.

We were sitting behind home plate, about twenty rows up, and there was a foul ball that flew over our heads. Immediately, I had the inclination to stand up and look back to where the ball was going. As I did, the ball ricocheted off the cement façade and came flying directly back at me. As I stood with my phone in one hand, I reached out my right hand and caught it!

The ball slammed into my palm, which slowed it down, popped up in the air and I grabbed it. I was so excited and could hardly believe it.

My daughter looked at me as I stood with the ball in my hand and simply said, "*Dad!*"

Back to the story. For Father's Day the past few years, my wife has saved up and surprised me in June by adding Root Sports to our list of channels we get so that I can watch Bucco baseball. I know, what a wife! For three to four months,

Liv and me at the ballgame

I get to catch a game here and there, but the problem is that it also comes with additional channels because you can't just order one. So, not only do I find myself at times watching the Pirates, but also some other shows, just because.

To be honest, even though I really enjoy catching some games, I'm always ready to turn it back to our basic channels once the time comes. Even if I watch one hour each night extra, that's seven hours or 420 minutes that week that I could have been doing something more productive.

Why is this chapter entitled, "*180 Minutes A Week*"?

Well, there is something we can do with just three hours a week that will help us in so many ways.

> "*Or do you not know that your body is the temple of the Holy Spirit who is in you, whom you have from God, and you are not your own? For you were bought at a price; therefore glorify God in your body and in your spirit, which are God's.*"
> —1 Corinthians 6:19-20

The Apostle Paul was reminding the Corinthians (and us today) that their bodies were a sanctuary where God dwells. Think of that! Our bodies are actually the spiritual dwelling place for God.

Let's look back at this verse in Exodus 40:34.

*"Then the cloud covered the tabernacle of meeting, and the glory of the LORD filled the tabernacle."*

Then we find in 1 Kings 8:10-11 these incredible words as the temple was completed.

*"And it came to pass, when the priests came out of the holy place, that the cloud filled the house of the LORD, so that the priests could not continue ministering because of the cloud; for the glory of the LORD filled the house of the LORD."*

Now combine these verses from the Old Testament with the verses we read from 1 Corinthians. We see that God's glory, through the Holy Spirit, now dwells within each and every believer and follower of Jesus Christ. And not only does He dwell there, but His power resides there! Here is what I believe is one of the most incredible verses in the Bible:

*"But if the Spirit of Him who raised Jesus from the dead dwells in you, He who raised Christ from the dead will also give life to your mortal bodies through His Spirit who dwells in you."*

—Romans 8:11

Jesus even reminded us of this as John wrote these words in his gospel:

*"And I pray the Father, and He will give you another Helper, that He may abide with you forever—*

*the Spirit of truth, whom the world cannot receive, because it neither sees Him nor knows Him; but you know Him, for He dwells with you and will be in you."*

—John 14:16-17

Now, I must preface what I'm about to say with this. Spiritual training and developing godliness in our lives should be our number one priority. But the *body and spirit* tend to go hand in hand if our bodies are the temple of the Holy Spirit. Even in the verses I just shared from 1 Corinthians 6, it says to *glorify God in your body **and** in your spirit.* I'm a firm believer that following spiritual training should come about 180 minutes of physical training and discipline.

Why? Well, there are many benefits to exercise.

I won't go into a long list of attributes when it comes to all the benefits, but exercise does keep you more alert, you feel better, you have more energy, you tend to be more creative, you waste less time, you work more efficiently and the bottom line is I believe it honors God. Why? Because His Spirit dwells within us.

I believe this is the stumbling block that arises with many who try to start an exercise routine. They try to do too much, too fast and can't keep up the pace and quit before they see many results. Physical exercise is a discipline that you must develop over time. It doesn't happen overnight, and don't try to go to the gym the first time, work out for hours, lift too much and not be able to move the next day. Sound familiar?

For most, that's not a pace you can keep. And to be honest, exercise can become an idol like anything else if we're not careful. Rather, simply try 180 minutes a week. That's all it really takes to develop a healthy exercise pattern in your life and experience some great benefits. Now this is more than building bigger muscles and trimming our waistlines. When you start to see exercise as a spiritual discipline, because remember, we are His temple, it begins to change your view of it because you want to take care of the place that God dwells, inside of you.

To go hand in hand with this are the things we like to eat. First, have you ever wondered why the things that are *good for us* taste, well, not so good? And the things that are *bad for us* taste, well, oh, so good?

One of my favorite foods is pizza and I really need to watch how much of it I consume. When I biked across the country on a mission trip a few years ago, one of my favorite things to find was a little pizza joint to give me some fuel. Actually, biking eight to ten hours a day allowed us to eat as much and anything we wanted and we still lost weight.

Harold, my bike riding partner, lost twenty pounds and I lost ten. I'm thankful to have what some call a *high metabolism*. It wasn't so fun when I was in high school and you wanted to put on some weight and have some muscle.

I remember even one teacher nicknaming me "the worm."

Another thing I remember him saying to me was that if I stood sideways and stuck out my tongue I'd look like a zipper. I know, nice teacher, huh? Really though, he was a pretty cool guy.

But I will say this, just because someone is thin, doesn't mean their insides are healthy. They may have a crazy metabolism that burns fat like water running down a duck's back, but their cholesterol may be high or their blood pressure could be through the roof. We must be careful of the things we place in our mouths, because eventually it will catch up with us over time in some shape or form.

Think of it this way, three hours per week over one year equals 156 hours, or six and a half days. If you exercise for fifty years of your life that equates to 325 days of your life. Keep this number in mind, 325 days, when I share more about what we do with our time in chapter eight.

Here are some practical tips to help make physical training a disciplined part of your week as you strive to carve out about 180 minutes into your schedule.

- Pick three days a week that you will regularly exercise. Stick to those days.
- Make the time on those days be right around the same part of the day.
- Make it easy to get to the gym you're going to or create a nice environment at home.

- Start with about twelve to eighteen minutes of cardiovascular exercise, followed by thirty to forty-five minutes of muscle building. Don't worry about gaining too much muscle, remember, muscle burns fat.
- If you are not able to join a gym or purchase equipment for home, take a long walk, ride a bike, or begin running.
- Drink lots of water. Most people don't drink enough and this really helps the body function well.

But once again, remember what Paul taught Timothy so that we keep this in perspective.

> *"For bodily exercise profits a little, but godliness is profitable for all things, having promise of the life that now is and of that which is to come."*
>
> —1 Timothy 4:8

Do both, but definitely place godliness and spiritual training first. Actually, looking at the verse just before this one reminds us that we are to *exercise yourself toward godliness.* As you do first things first, your temple where His Spirit dwells will begin to feel different and you will want to add some physical training. As you do this, your physical training will begin to feel like spiritual training as well. You will begin to desire the things of the spirit rather than the flesh.

Let's work on our temples . . . for Jesus truly deserves our very best and a beautiful house to live in.

## CHAPTER 3 - SMALL GROUP DISCUSSION

**Read 1 Corinthians 6:19-20.**

- Have you ever considered that your body is the *temple of the Holy Spirit?*
- How should this affect the way we live our lives and what we do with our time?

**Read Romans 8:11 and John 14:16-17.**

- How does the fact that His Spirit lives in you affect your daily living?
- How can I begin to make *bodily training* a part of my lifestyle?
- What practical things can I do to make this a priority in my life?
- Is it possible to look at physical training as part of your spiritual training in some ways? If so, how?

# Next To Jesus

### NEXT TO JESUS, WHAT'S NEXT?

In chapter two, I shared how Jesus deserves top billing in our lives. The Scriptures even make this clear as the Holy Spirit inspired the Apostle Paul to write Philippians 2:9-11.

> *"Therefore God also has highly exalted Him and given Him the name which is above every name,*
>
> *that at the name of Jesus every knee should bow, of those in heaven, and of those on earth, and of those under the earth,*
>
> *and that every tongue should confess that Jesus Christ is Lord, to the glory of God the Father."*

It was our Heavenly Father's pleasure and desire to give Jesus the Name that is higher than any other name there ever has been or will be. Don't be misled, there is no other name that is greater, more powerful and also more controversial than Jesus. The fact still remains, the name of Jesus still offends many. From the moment He took that first breath in that lowly stable, people wanted to kill Him.

Could you imagine people wanting to kill you from the very first day of your life? Even today, do you notice how the name of Jesus stirs the pot? Oh, you can say the name *God* and people don't get too excited, and it is very acceptable in society. Not to get political, but even those who run for office, whether they seem to be followers of Christ, or not, say *"God bless America, "or "God bless you."*

Why doesn't this get people wound up? Well, because most people believe that as long as you worship a god, we're all on the same page and we're all going to heaven. So when the name of God is spoken, people receive it and even applaud.

Could you imagine if a politician ended one of his or her speeches with this, "Jesus loves you, "or "May Jesus bless and keep you."

Talk about headline news!

What offends people and is a stumbling block for many is still the name of Jesus. The One True Lord God Almighty said it would be this way. He is the One who gave His only begotten Son the Name above every name. It was God's plan from the very beginning. Jesus the name above every name.

What offends many is that the Bible makes it perfectly clear that He is the only way to heaven and this to many seems very intolerant and exclusive. Well, here is what Jesus said and others declared in the Scripture:

*"I am the way, the truth, and the life. No one comes to the Father except through Me."* Jesus, John 14:6

*"But we preach Christ crucified, to the Jews a stumbling block and to the Greeks foolishness."* Paul, 1 Corinthians 1:23

*"For we are to God the fragrance of Christ among those who are being saved and among those who are perishing.
To the one we are the aroma of death leading to death, and to other the aroma of life leading to life. And who is sufficient for these things?"* Paul, 2 Corinthians 2:15-16

We even learn by reading John 1:1-3 what a crucial part Jesus played in creation.

*"In the beginning was the Word, and the Word was with God, and the Word was God. He was in the beginning with God. All things were made through Him, and without Him nothing was made that was made."*

Then in John 1:14 it states, *"And the Word became flesh and dwelt among us."*

These verses show us how the Word is Jesus and how God sent His Son in the flesh to dwell amongst us. So, when Genesis 1:1 starts with these three same words, *"In the beginning,"* where was Jesus?

Right there with God.

Without Jesus, nothing would have been created. Before Jesus came to earth, He was by His Father in heaven. Then one day, God sent His only Son to earth, for us. The timing of Him coming to earth was perfect. The world was a mess, the world needed a Savior, and God sent His Son, Jesus. And He gave Him the Name above every name.

*"For God so loved the world that He gave His only begotten Son, that whoever believes in Him should not perish but have everlasting life."*

—John 3:16

Jesus must become everything to us. If He isn't everything, is He really anything?

He must not be simply a baby in a manger that we set up once a year in the yard or remember on Easter Sunday. He must become our master, our best friend, the One we seek for everything.

Everything? Yes, everything!

Where I live? Yep. Where I work? Uh-huh. How about where I bank, shop and what gym I exercise at? Uh, yeah, those too. Where I go to college, where I spend my money, my free time, who I marry, and my . . . life? Yes, everything. Jesus desires to be a part of anything and everything we do. Are you up for that?

The name of this chapter, "Next to Jesus," represents the very reason Jesus came to earth, He came for people. Think about it, if there were never any people on the earth, He would have never needed to leave His Father's side.

Peter writes about the heartbeat of Christ in this verse:

*"The Lord is not slack concerning His promise, as some count slackness, but is longsuffering toward us, not willing that any should perish but that all should come to repentance."*

—2 Peter 3:9

It is the Lord's desire that all would come to repentance, not simply just believe in God. You see, James, who was the half-brother of Jesus but introduces himself to us in his letter as a *bondservant of God and the Lord Jesus Christ*, reminds us of this:

*"You believe that there is one God. You do well. Even the demons believe—and tremble!"*

—James 2:19

To look at the previous verse from Peter in another way, to not perish, we must come to that point of repentance in our lives. Repentance means to *turn away*.

Turn away from what? From sin.

The writer of Hebrews reminds us how sin can so easily entangle our hearts and lives:

*"Therefore we also, since we are surrounded by so great a cloud of witnesses, let us lay aside every weight, and the sin which so easily ensnares us, and let us run with endurance the race that is set before us,*

*looking unto Jesus, the author and finisher of our faith, who for the joy set before Him endured the cross, despising the shame, and has sat down at the right hand of the throne of God."*

—Hebrews 12:1-2

The reason Jesus came was to ultimately die for our sins and reconcile us back into a right relationship with God that was severely broken. Jesus mended our relationship with God, and the very heartbeat of Jesus today is still about people. Next to Jesus, the most important part of our lives should be people and the relationships we're blessed to have around us. If not careful, we can very easily get caught up into thinking of three things in life: *me, myself, and I.*

For years, a simple prayer of mine had been (in this order): *"Lord, help me to be, first, the man of God you have called me to be, second the husband, third the father and fourth the pastor."*

You see, I believe that if I'm not being the first three, I might as well not attempt to be the fourth one because I would be ineffective and as my dad used to say, a "phony baloney."

If you are in full-time ministry, we must make sure our priorities are in the right order. What I've found is that when I'm first and foremost seeking Him, then working to be a good husband and father, then I can be effective to the people that God has called me to shepherd.

For years I prayed this prayer, but within the past few years, the Lord showed me something I was missing in this prayer of mine. It is a very important aspect of our lives and one we are called to love just as much as ourselves.

So here is what I added.

*"Lord, help me to be the man of God You have called me to be, the husband, the father, the **neighbor** and the pastor."*

My neighbor! To truly be who Christ has called us to be we must love our neighbors. Not just those who live next door to us, even though that is a great place to start, but those we rub shoulders with every day at the workplace, in the marketplace, and wherever we find ourselves on a regular basis.

Let's remember what Jesus said when one of the scribes came and asked Him the question, "Which is the greatest commandment of all?"

Now we usually focus on the two commandments that Jesus gives this scribe, which are amazing. Maybe you can say them without reading them, but here they are.

Jesus said, *" . . . you shall love the Lord your God with all your heart, with all your soul, with all your mind, and with all your strength . . . and the second, like it, is this: You shall love your neighbor as yourself."*

Then Jesus made this statement, *"There is no other commandment greater than these."*

Let's back up for a moment. The one who asked Jesus the question to begin with was a scribe, who was a student of the Law of Moses. In other words, he knew the Old Testament Law. In a way, he was putting Jesus to the test to see just how much He knew about the Law and which of the commandments was actually the greatest. By the way, this can be found in Mark 12 and Matthew 22.

Jesus begins His answer with this, *"Hear, O Israel, the Lord our God, the Lord is one."*

The phrase, "Hear, O Israel," in Hebrew is referred to as the "Shema." The meaning of the word is simple, "to hear."

This had to get their attention! How Jesus begins His answer is the exact same phrase found in Deuteronomy 6:4 which says, *"Hear, O Israel: The LORD our God, the LORD is one!"*

Before I go further with this thought, let's look at the two things that we see Jesus said are the greatest commandments:

> *Love the Lord your God with all your heart, with all your soul,*
> *with all your mind, and with all your strength.*
> *Love your neighbor as yourself.*

Love your neighbor as who? Yourself.

Could it be that it is so hard to love our neighbors because we don't really even like who we are when we look in the mirror? On my recent bike mission trip on Route 66 called "Mission 66 . . . If My People," I ran into a guy that felt he did so much wrong that he could never possibly be forgiven and loved by Christ. I must say it saddened my heart as I pedaled away following our conversation.

The Bible tells us:

> *"There is therefore now no condemnation to those who are in Christ Jesus,*
> *who do not walk according to the flesh, but according to the Spirit."*
> —Romans 8:1

Jesus truly does want you to live in freedom, not under condemnation from your past. But we must not walk according to our flesh to find that freedom, but rather according to the Spirit. Christ has provided His Spirit to influence our walk every day. He wants us to walk in freedom and begin to love who we are. Not in a narcissistic way, but in a healthy way that allows us to find who we are in Christ, walk in His love, love ourselves, and then begin to love our neighbors. You and I know, it's very hard to love people at times. That's why we need His love to do so.

Read what David wrote about his experience in coming to know how much God loved him:

*"For You formed my inward parts; You covered me in my mother's womb.*
*I will praise You, for I am fearfully and wonderfully made;*
*Marvelous are your works, And that my soul knows very well."*
—Psalm 139:13-14

I encourage you to take a moment and read that entire chapter in your Bible. David, who needed to know God's forgiveness in a mighty way, knew how loved he was. It actually says that his soul knew it very well. I believe as we begin to experience just how much God loves us, we will experience the freedom to walk under His grace and His love, and then begin to love not only ourselves, but others around us.

There is something else that Jesus did here that summarized the Ten Commandments. Was this scribe really wanting to pick one of these ten as the greatest?

Jesus broke up the "Top Ten" into two categories, the first four with regard to how we *love the Lord*, and five through ten with how we *love our neighbors*.

Check this out:

| Love the Lord your God | Love your neighbor |
|---|---|
| C #1: No other gods | C #5: Honor your father and mother |
| C #2: No carved images | C #6: Do not murder |
| C #3: Don't take the Lord's name in vain | C #7: Do not commit adultery |
| C #4: Remember the Sabbath | C #8: Do not steal |
|  | C #9: Do not bear false witness |
|  | C #10: Don't covet anything of your neighbor |

Do any of you, like me, find it hard to wrap your mind around this and actually do what Jesus says to do? Did you notice that little three letter word He used in answering the scribe, "all"? To love God will *all* our heart, soul, mind, and strength. To me this means holding nothing back.

What would this truly look like in my life? And then, on top of that, I'm called to love my neighbor as myself. Umm, wow! So how do we do this, and why is it that we can fall woefully short of this in our lives at times? I mean, we may say we do, but are we really?

The only way to do this is to recognize what Jesus said before He gave these two greatest commandments. It's the key in living these out and without it, we won't be able to do the most important things that Jesus calls us to do.

Let's go back to Mark 12 and see once again how Jesus began His answer to this scribe.

*"Jesus answered him, 'The first of all commandments is: Hear, O
Israel, the LORD our God, the LORD is one.'"*
—Mark 12:29

He then went on to say, *"And you shall love the LORD your God with all
your heart, with all your soul, with all your mind, and with all your strength.
This is the first commandment. And the second, like it, is this: You shall love
your neighbor as yourself"* (Mark 12:30-31a).

I believe what Jesus is saying here is that unless we set apart the
Lord and make Him number One in our lives, we will never be able
to fulfill the two greatest commandments. We must remember who
Jesus was speaking to, the Israelites and students of the Law. Again, the
phrase, *"Hear, O Israel,"* (Shema) had to get their attention, but notice
He spoke it right after (not before) He said, *"the first of all commandments is."* Jesus was saying first, *"listen up . . . the Lord has to be first, tops,
number one in your life. If He is, you will be able to do what I'm about to tell
you."* We must worship the One and only One God in our lives. I'm
not talking about all the gods of different religions in the world. The
Bible teaches us that there is only One True God. But how many have
gods called *'work, hobbies, sports, shopping, food, sex, obsessions, addictions,
money, social media'* and a host of other things that can take the place
of the One True God? I believe that one day when we stand before the
Lord, our time, our schedules and our money will either speak for or
against us. These tend to prove who our One True God really is. The
Lord convicted my heart about this a few years back when He shined
a light on these verses and said in so many words,

> *"K.R., you cannot love Me with all your heart, soul, mind and
> strength and also love your neighbor as yourself until you set Me
> apart as your One True God and have no other gods before Me."*

It was then that I began to strive after this in my heart. And you
know as well as I do, it's a battle we must face and conquer every day.
But let's dig a little deeper, why did Jesus start with this? Well, the

scribe knew the commandments and just asked Jesus which one (of the ten) was the greatest, right? Look back again at what commandment number one is?

> *"You shall have no other gods before Me."*
>
> —Exodus 20:3

And that's exactly where Jesus began:

> *'Hear, O Israel, the LORD our God, the LORD is one."*
>
> —Mark 12:29b

Still holds true today. We must make sure we have set the Lord apart in our hearts and declare Him to be number One. If we do, the next part will flow from our lives. The relationships *"next to Jesus"* will be healthy, strong, and vibrant. Our relationships next to Jesus will begin to be a very real example of what it looks like to have the Lord as number One in our lives. We must take time, seek and love Jesus first, and make Him Lord over our entire life. He wants to be both Savior and Lord. There is a difference. The word Savior is referred to in the New Testament sixteen times and the reference to Lord is made over 400 times. Jesus did come to die, forgive us of our sins, and be our <u>Savior</u>. But He also came to then fulfill His purposes in our lives as Lord. I really don't think it's possible to have one without the other, because in Romans 10:9 Paul writes,

> *"That if you confess with your mouth the Lord Jesus and believe in your heart that God has raised Him from the dead, you will be saved."*

And then in verse 13 he says,

> *"For 'whoever calls on the name of the LORD shall be saved.'"*

So many want heaven later, but how many are willing to submit to Him as Lord now? Jesus, may You truly be our Lord, our One true God, so that we can begin to love You in the proper way and then love others around us as you flow through our lives. Next to You Jesus, help us to love our spouses, our children, our families, our neighbors, and yes, even our enemies. Help us to not get angry with people who are rude, arrogant or inconsiderate. Help us to love them as you loved us *while we were still sinners,"* (Romans 5:8). Oh, Jesus, next to You may our time be invested in people, because that's why You came. For us!

## CHAPTER 4 - SMALL GROUP DISCUSSION

Next to Jesus, we must begin to develop relationships with people. Why is this so important in our walk with Christ?

What gets in the way of setting apart the *"One True God"* as the only God in our lives?

**Read Mark 12:29-31.**

Is it possible to fulfill these two greatest commandments without making the Lord number One in our lives?

Jesus said to "love our neighbors as ourselves." After reading **Psalm 139:1-16**, would you say it's possible that we don't love our neighbors because we really don't like who we are?

- If so, how can we begin to be set free from our past and begin to accept how loved we are by the Lord God Almighty?
- **Read Romans 8:1.** Christ has paid the price for our freedom. According to this verse, what must we be sure we are doing so that we don't live under condemnation any longer?

## CHAPTER 5

# Right or Left?

I VIVIDLY REMEMBER SATURDAY MORNINGS as a kid, waking up early, grabbing a bowl of cereal, and settling in front of our television to watch cartoons. I remember when it was a chilly morning wrapping up in a blanket and just enjoying the comedy that came from these simple, yet innocent, cartoons. That time seems so long ago growing up in Springdale, Pennsylvania, on 325 Moyhend Street.

Some of my favorite cartoons were *Looney Tunes*—Bugs Bunny, The Roadrunner and who could forget Foghorn Leghorn. Then there was Hong Kong Phooey. Just how did that janitor get changed in that file cabinet?

I remember a phrase from one of the shows where a character would say, *"Which way did he go, George?"*

The show was called *Of Fox and Hounds.* The dog's name was Willoughby and the fox's, George. In the scene I watched online recently to refresh my memory of the show, Willoughby was asking George if he had seen a fox pass by and if he knew which way he went. George begins to give directions as to which way the fox, which was himself, went. On a side note, one reason I can't wait to have grandkids is so that I can introduce them to what *real cartoons* are all about!

But how many of us ask this same question day in and day out, *which way should I go?*

There are so many decisions to be made every day and in the big scope of things, major decisions like whether or not to go to college, if and whom we're to marry, where we are to live and so on that will affect so many things in our lives.

*"Which way should we go, which way should we turn? Should I go right, or turn left? What decision should I make—they both seem like good choices."*

These are questions I think we all face every day. What becomes really difficult is when we have to make a decision between two good choices.

I remember almost twenty years ago when my wife and I had to choose between remaining at a successful ministry at our home church just outside of Pittsburgh, Pennsylvania, or moving on to another position in State College, Pennsylvania. It was a very difficult decision between two very good choices.

What we did was simply pray and seek the Lord for direction as to what He would have us to do. The other huge thing that convinced my heart as to what we were to do was to choose some Scripture verses to stand upon. As we did this, I remember hearing these verses used in some messages that I heard that convinced our hearts that we were making the right decision to move on to State College. I look back and realize how much we would have missed if we had stayed where we were. But I also believe that if we had stayed, He would have continued to use us in ministry there in new ways as well.

If we simply seek the Lord through prayer and His Word, He will lead us. And if we seek to make the very best decisions we can as we listen for His voice leading us, even if we may *miss it,* here and there, eventually I believe He will make our paths turn out exactly how He intended.

It reminds me of Proverbs 3:5-6:

*"Trust in the LORD with all your heart, And lean not on your own understanding;*
*In all your ways acknowledge Him, And He shall direct your paths."*

When it comes to making decisions, we must realize that if we are a believer and follower of Jesus Christ, He has not abandoned us to make these decisions on our own. One of the prophesies that I love in the Old Testament is the fact that even before Christ came, it was prophesied that He would be our Wonderful, Counselor.

*"For unto us a Child is born,*

*Unto us a Son is given;*

*And the government will be upon His shoulder.*

*And His name will be called Wonderful, Counselor, Mighty God, Everlasting Father, Prince of Peace."*

—Isaiah 9:6

Now, as believers, there are good counselors and bad counselors. We must be careful whose counsel we choose to seek, listen to, and follow. But when Jesus came to earth and as He was preparing to leave, we must keep in mind something He said that is very important to remember when making decisions.

*"These things I have spoken to you while being present with you.*

*But the Helper, the Holy Spirit, whom the Father will send in My name, He will teach you all things, and bring to your remembrance all things that I said to you."*

—John 14:25-26

Now, we know that the Holy Spirit lives in us, and there are times throughout our minutes every day that He wants to teach us something. But are we listening? I mean, if you are like me, our days can become so full that we sometimes fly by the seat of our pants.

Can anyone relate? But Jesus is wanting us to hear His voice in the midst of our moments every day. I believe the clearest way that the Lord speaks to us is through His Word. It is His story to us.

Have you ever had someone say to you (or maybe you've said it yourself), *"I wish the Lord would just speak to me!"*

If that's you or you know someone who has said that to you, remind them that the Bible is God's inspired Word and has been breathed into existence to give you His direction for your life. His Word is powerful and it was inspired by the Holy Spirit, which lives where? Inside of us.

I believe that when we read the Holy Spirit-inspired Word of God, it activates our faith inside of us and we begin to hear Him more clearly. It's like the Holy Spirit begins to cut through the noise and distractions of our days.

The writer of Hebrews reminds us how powerful the Word is when the Holy Spirit inspired the writer to write these words:

> *"For the word of God is living and powerful, and sharper than any two-edged sword, piercing even to the division of soul and spirit, and of joints and marrow, and is a discerner of the thoughts and intents of the heart."*

> —Hebrews 4:12

Can you think of anything else that can accomplish in our lives what you just read? God's Word is living, powerful, and sharper than any two-edged sword.

When our son, Luke, finished reading the Bible as a teenager, I bought him a sword to hang on his wall. I wanted him to know that there is nothing that can shape and direct your life like the Word of God. And on top of that, as you read earlier in John 1:1, Jesus is the Word and when we spend time digesting it, the Holy Spirit takes it and begins to teach us all things.

*Which way should we go?*

Well, as followers of Jesus Christ we have a Teacher, a Wonderful Counselor living inside of us that desires to direct our steps every minute and with every single heartbeat of our lives. As human beings we have decisions that we need to make every day. We usually have a plan, or path, for our lives that we're formulating in our minds. But have we given room for the Lord to change those plans? Are we listening to the voice of the Holy Spirit that may be wanting to direct us in a different way? Are we set on our course and have we blocked out His voice from overriding us?

The question we all must ask ourselves is, *"Who is in charge? Me or Him?"*

I think we all want to say Him, but shouldn't we stop and ask, *"Is He really? Or am I just doing my own thing and inviting Him along to bless my plans?"*

Are they really His plans for my life? If we can't emphatically say *yes*, then we must lay ourselves and our lives before Him and ask, *"Which way should I turn next?"*

Just remember, take one step at a time.  And never forget:

*"A man's heart plans his way, But the LORD directs his steps."*

—Proverbs 16:9

When I made the big decision to go into full time ministry in 1996, it was one that both my wife and I sought the Lord about in prayer. When we moved to State College to become the Children's Pastor in 1999, we prayed for direction again and I remember the Lord giving me Scripture to confirm in our hearts that this was *His next step* for our lives.

I won't go into details here, but needless to say, both of those moves included sacrifices that we had to make to follow His will rather than our own. But they were worth it! We were really being careful to try and listen to His voice speak loud and clear into our lives. Looking back, we would not have accomplished so much for the Lord had we never sold the business we owned in 1996, and then our home we built in 1999 to move, what seemed to our kids, I'm sure, a million miles away.

You know as well as I do that comfort rarely equates growth. Usually, comfort will keep us from spending our minutes on what God intends for us to accomplish. We must do something very difficult to begin to hear His voice, saying, *"Turn right, go left ... no this way, up this hill, go straight."*

Here is what it comes down to, we must be willing to ...

> *" ... present your bodies a living sacrifice, holy, acceptable to God, which is your reasonable service.*
>
> *And do not be conformed to this world, but be transformed by the renewing of your mind, that you may prove what is that good and acceptable and perfect will of God."*
>
> —Romans 12:1-2

Who doesn't want to know *God's perfect will* for their lives? The real question becomes, are we willing to lay down our lives as a sacrifice to get it? Notice if we do what is said in these verses, we will be able to prove what His good, acceptable, and perfect will is for our lives. Who doesn't want that? But are we really willing to pay the price? Remember when Abraham took Isaac up the mountain to sacrifice his son? Isaac was the promised child and his dad's most treasured possession. And God wanted to see if He was willing to lay it down as a sacrifice. Abraham had to listen and then respond to the voice of God.

What if Abraham would have never climbed that mountain? So true in our lives, as well, if we want to present ourselves as living sacrifices and do whatever He asks of us. It may go against anything you ever saw yourself doing or becoming, but it's His plan for your life, not your own. Sacrifice hurts, there is pain, and it takes a killing of our flesh to become a living sacrifice so that we can hear more clearly from His Spirit deep within us. As we sacrifice our lives though, we will then begin to hear His voice with more sensitivity because we are getting the flesh out of the way.

Another thing that helps in this process is fasting. It truly does begin to kill our flesh. Do you want to know God's will? Who doesn't?

Sometimes we tend to complicate the process of finding His will like it is some hidden treasure. His will is not some mystery to be solved, rather it is an unfolding in our lives one step at a time as we become more obedient to His Word.

Don't try to figure out His will for the next twenty years, just take the next step, the next heartbeat, the next minute. As you do, the Lord will direct you into His perfect will for your life.  I love what Paul reminds us is God's will for our lives.

> "Be joyful always;
> pray continually;
> give thanks in all circumstances, for this is God's will for you in Christ Jesus."
> —1 Thessalonians 5:16-18 (NIV)

*God's will focus* [handwritten note in margin]

This is a simple explanation of what God's will is for our lives. Be joyful (always), pray (continually), give thanks (in all circumstances). Pretty simple formula, but so hard to put into practice. That is what Paul says is God's will for your life as you give your life as a living sacrifice.

And if we do these things, even in the hardest of times, we will continue to find His will unfold before us as we stay grounded in His Word every day. Take note of what the Lord wants to do for us as we begin to realize He is speaking to us.

Here is one of my favorite verses in the Bible:

> "Your ears shall hear a word behind you, saying,
> 'This is the way, walk in it,'
> Whenever you turn to the right hand
> Or whenever you turn to the left."
> —Isaiah 30:21

Now this does not mean that you are going to hear an audible voice, but rather as you spend time in God's Word, you will begin to hear the Holy Spirit's voice bring to your remembrance the Word as you go through your days. And the more time you spend in God's Word, the more sensitive you will become to the Holy Spirit's voice.

Some of you reading this book right now are at a crossroads in your life? Not sure what to do with your minutes that really matter? You have some big decisions ahead. May I encourage you not to be afraid to do what He is asking you to do and leave the results in His hands? You may not like it, it may hurt, and it may be way out of your comfort zone. But if He says, *"go right, turn left, go this way,"* then do it.

Be sure, pray it through, spend time in His Word . . . and then go for it! I know that you will make the right decision if you pray and spend time in His Word because it reminds us in Isaiah 55:11:

> *"So shall My Word be that goes forth from My mouth;*
> *It shall not return to me void.*
> *But it shall accomplish what I please.*
> *And it shall prosper in the thing for which I sent it."*

I remember praying through before committing to bike across America a few years ago on a mission trip called *Coast 2 Coast 4 Jesus.* I did not tell anyone for quite some time what I was thinking and praying about, not even my wife. I wanted to be sure that it was the Lord speaking to me and not just a harebrained idea of mine which I tend to have from time to time.

A joke between my wife and I is that I'm this guy in the air holding onto a helium balloon, while she is on the ground hanging onto my ankle so that I don't drift away too far. We balance each other well.

But I knew that if I shared my biking across America idea before I had prayed and spent time seeking the Lord for confirmation, that I could have been talked out of this pretty easily. I also knew that many would probably think I was losing my mind, even though that may be true at times. Through His Word, prayer, and journaling what the Lord was speaking to my heart, He confirmed that, yes, I was to bike across America for Jesus.

You can find out more about this entire story in the book, *Don't Quit* (www.rocknrollministries.com).

But I recall standing in the kitchen and first sharing with my wife about what I believe the Lord wanted me to do. I don't know what was rolling around in her head as she stared at me, but I remember her words, *"If you know the Lord wants you to do it, then do it."* What a wife!

At the same time, there were ones who questioned this decision. So, who was I to listen to? Well, the key for me was that my decision was already made before I asked or told anyone else.

The Lord convinced my heart during those few weeks of prayer and seeking Him, and He will do the same for you no matter how big or small of a decision you have to make.

Our minutes truly do matter. Let's just remember to leave room for Him to direct your steps, even as we plan our way.

Remember this verse, it's worth repeating.

*"A man's heart plans his way, But the LORD directs his steps."*
—Proverbs 16:9

Tune and train your ear to hear His voice. He still speaks today because His Word remains faithful and His Spirit is still living within us. Ignite that Spirit in you with the fuel of His Word, and watch Him direct your steps in ways you never thought possible.

Hang on, it's a great journey! Challenging, hard, sometimes life-threatening? Possibly. But, oh, so worth it!

## CHAPTER 5 - SMALL GROUP DISCUSSION

Have you ever had a decision to make between two good choices? How did you decide which choice to make?

**Read Hebrews 4:12.**

- How powerful does it say God's Word is to accomplish so much in our lives?

**Read Romans 12:1-2 and 1 Thessalonians 5:16-18.**

- What do these verses say we should be doing to find God's will in our lives? How am I doing at these right now?

How often during your days do you find yourself asking the Lord for direction or wisdom?

How can we become more in-tune, more in step, with the Holy Spirit?

# CHAPTER 6

# Whatever

HAVE YOU EVER HEARD SOMEONE put an end to a conversation by saying, "whatever!"?

It usually isn't a very endearing word to use in this way and is probably spoken with a sharp tone in the voice. Imagine with me the following conversation . . .

Wife: Did you pick up the milk from the store that I asked you to get?

Husband: You asked me to pick up milk from the store?

Wife: Yes, don't you remember? Before you left this morning I said we were out of milk.

Husband: I know, but you didn't say that you wanted me to pick some up.

Wife: Do I have to spell everything out to you? *(And all the husbands right now are saying . . . YES!)*

Husband: Well, it sure would help.

Wife: OK, next time I will set the empty milk carton on the passenger seat of the car with a sign on it that says, "GET MILK ON THE WAY HOME!"

Husband: Whatever! *(and the husband ends up on the couch for the night).*

Now, first of all, my wife and I have been married for almost 30 years and you would think that communication would get easier, not harder. Secondly, the above conversation is not between my wife and me. However, we have had other interesting dialogues over the years that seem like we are on two totally different planets trying to discuss one topic using three different languages . . . hers, mine and the "what in the world are you talking about" language that we both can't seem to understand. I'll keep those ones to myself since I don't want to sleep on the couch tonight.

When someone says *whatever* in this manner, it is usually done with frustration and a lack of interest to continue the conversation. At that point, the discussion (if that's what you want to call it) usually ends with no resolution or escalates even further because the other may respond with something like, *"you never listen to me."*

But this word can also be used in a very positive way. We are going to begin this chapter by looking at two places in Scripture where this word is used to describe how we are to do whatever we do and to remember who we are ultimately doing it for.

*"And whatever you do in word or deed, do all in the name of the*
*Lord Jesus, giving thanks to God the Father through Him."*
—Colossians 3:17

*"And whatever you do, do it heartily, as to the Lord and not to men,*
*knowing that from the Lord you will receive the reward of the*
*inheritance; for you serve the Lord Christ."*
—Colossians 3:23-24

To grasp the entire meaning of these verses, we must look at the verses around them. Keep in mind when reading Scripture that when written, there were no separations by verse and chapter numbers. Each book simply flowed together as one continual letter. So, taking a look before and after these verses, you will find different groups of people that these verses were referring to. Wives, husbands, children, fathers, bondservants, masters; but ultimately it refers to simply all those who are following Jesus Christ with their lives.

May I encourage you to take time and read Colossians 3 before you continue reading the rest of this chapter?

If we are to truly make our *minutes matter*, it is absolutely critical that we remember who we are doing *whatever* we do for. Ultimately, everything we do should be done through the lens of the cross and with Christ in mind. If we serve in a way and are doing it for some person rather than for Christ, we may quit and give up. But if whatever we do we keep in mind that we are serving Christ, then our serving will be a joy and we won't give up because we are choosing to serve Christ and not man.

Here is a story that reminded me of this application of Scripture. In 2004, my family planted a church in a beautiful region of central Pennsylvania called Penns Valley. For ten years we met in a school where we had to pull in a trailer that held our equipment, unload it, set it up, and then tear it down and pack it up into the trailer. Seven days later, we would do it again. Five hundred and twenty times we would repeat this process over the ten years.

I remember my wife towards the end of that time in our ministry saying something along these lines, *"If you would have told me in the beginning that we would've done this for ten years I'm not sure I would've signed up."*

But the reason that we survived and did not quit was because we had a great team of people that understood the concept of serving the Lord and not serving K.R. and Gina Mele.

One team member would faithfully move the trailer in each weekend for years. I would express my thanks to him for doing so, and each time he would respond to me with these words, *"I'm not doing it for you, I'm doing it for the Lord."*

I LOVED THAT! I told him that I'm so glad he feels this way because if he were doing it for me he would eventually quit. But if you do something for the Lord, you keep going.

I began this book with the verse from Psalm 90:12 which says, *"So teach us to number our days, That we may gain a heart of wisdom."*

When we ask to be taught, it is because we need to learn something. I don't know about you, but the older I get, the more I seem to be learning and the wiser I think I'm becoming (except on certain days when I forget to pick up the milk, but, whatever).

But doesn't that go along with the verse in Proverbs that says: *"The silver-haired head is a crown of glory, If it is found in the way of righteousness."*

—Proverbs 16:31

This is a verse where you have to read the second half to truly understand the first part. Our lives must be found in the way of righteousness, and if it is, as our hair turns silver, it will be our crown of glory. You may hear some refer to grey hair being a crown of glory, but they leave the second part out.

How many of you know people who have grown old and have grey hair? Does that grey hair automatically make it a crown of glory? No, both the Godly and ungodly have grey hair, but it's only when a life is found in the way of righteousness that their silver hair can then be known as their crown of glory.

Too often this happens with Scripture as half a verse is used and the full meaning of the Word begins to be misused and interpreted in wrong ways. Here is just one example of that, and then I'll get back to *whatever!*

How many of you have ever heard someone say, *"resist the devil and he will flee from you"*? True? Well, yes, but only if the first part of this verse is combined with it.

The entirety of this verse found in James 4:7 says this: *"Therefore submit to God. Resist the devil and he will flee from you."*

How many people are trying to *"resist the devil and asking him to flee from them,"* but their lives are far from being submitted to God? You see, we can't have one without the other. We can't resist the devil without our lives being submitted to God. But when this verse is used in its entirety, it's powerful!

When a life is totally and completely surrendered to God, the devil doesn't stand a chance. When we resist him, he must flee. We must

make sure our lives are submitted to God, and that the power of the Holy Spirit is living in us, if that is true, resist away and the devil has no choice but to flee from you.

Do you know what the devil wants? He does not want us to read or understand Scripture, but a sly trick of his is to also try and cause us to misuse the Word or use only parts of it and not the full authority of God's Word. That is what he did when he tried to tempt Jesus in the desert. Remember? This is how it happened as Matthew wrote about one of these temptations in his Gospel.

> *"Then the devil took Him up into the holy city, set Him on the pinnacle of the temple,*
>
> *and said to Him, 'If You are the Son of God, throw Yourself down. For it is written: 'He shall give His angels charge over you,' and 'In their hands they shall bear you up, Lest you dash your foot against a stone.'*
>
> *Jesus said to him, 'It is written again, 'You shall not tempt the LORD your God.'"*
>
> —Matthew 4:5-7

The devil quoted a verse from the Old Testament, but left out part of it. He also took a verse and built a theological stance around it. Be careful when you hear of people or ministries that do this.

Here is the verse in its entirety.

> *"For He shall give His angels charge over you, To keep you in all your ways.*
>
> *In their hands they shall bear you up, Lest you dash your foot against a stone."*
>
> —Psalm 91:11-12

Here's the point: We must know the Word inside and out, because the devil knows the Word himself and will try to twist it, omit things, change it or simply try and diminish its power in our lives.

Whatever . . . whatever we do—being a mom, dad, husband, wife, child, brother, sister, employer, employee—make those minutes matter by doing *whatever* we do while always keeping the Lord in mind.

Let's break down these two verses like this.

And WHATEVER you do:

- in word or deed (what we say or what we do)

- do all in the name of the Lord Jesus (you are representing Him every minute of your day)

- giving thanks to God the Father through Him (thank Him, because it's all about Him, as He is the one who has blessed you with the ability to do what you do)

And WHATEVER you do:

- do it heartily (work hard at what you do)

- as to the Lord and not to men (remember, ultimately you are working for the Lord, honor Him)

- knowing that from the Lord you will receive the reward of the inheritance (your reward is not your paycheck or lack of it, your reward is your inheritance of eternal life) and His presence in your life

- for you serve the Lord Christ (He should be our ultimate authority on all the things we say or do)

When I look at my life, and as my hair does begin to turn grey, I'm trying to reflect on my minutes and if *whatever I do*, I'm remembering to do them unto the Lord and ask Him, *"Does this please You?"*

I recently passed the fifty year mark of my life, which equates to 26,280,000 minutes that I've been blessed with since my very first breath on November 13, 1966. Isn't it true (if you are reading this and the grey hairs are popping up in your head, too), that when we were younger, we thought we knew all the answers to life?

But as you serve the Lord, wisdom does come and you begin to understand more and more about what life is all about. When I visit the "silver saints" in their homes or the nursing homes, I love to hear their stories. Being a generation ahead of me, they have so much to offer (and they make me feel younger than I am).

If I happen to visit older ones who don't know the Lord, they usually don't have as much wisdom to offer. Actually, they seem to have stories to tell, but not as much wisdom. But when I sit with one who has served the Lord, been in His Word and lived it out, they are a joy to sit with and learn from.

One dear lady and friend that I love to visit is eighty-eight-year-old, Evelyn. She has read through her Bible eleven times and still reads every day as she heads towards number twelve. Her faithfulness to the Lord and her knowledge from the Word has allowed her to live a life of righteousness and so her silver head can be called a *crown of glory*. I had the great privilege to baptize her in the Coburn creek in Penns Valley about eight years ago when she was eighty.

I'll never forget her two grandsons walking with her down into the water. Even at eighty, she wanted to walk closer to the Lord. And still at eighty-eight, she makes reading the Word a part of her daily routine. I consider Evelyn a friend of mind and a "whatever" type of lady.

Evelyn and me

Whatever she does, she desires to do it unto the Lord. I've had the privilege to make homemade bread with her at her home a couple of times. I cannot begin to tell you what a blessing those hours were. Here are some pictures of one our days spent together making bread.

Evelyn, thank you for your faithfulness to the Lord and allowing your life of righteousness to make your head a crown of glory. Oh, the stories I could tell of all my visits with her in the small house she lives in tucked up against a mountain and Amish homes in Central

Pennsylvania between Aaronsburg and Woodward.

But I'll leave you with this about Evelyn. She has lived her days, not for herself, but for the Lord and those she served in His name. Whatever she did, she did with a grateful heart,

worked heartily and realized it really wasn't about herself. I believe she simply placed other people before herself. I wish everyone could have an Evelyn in their life. I've been blessed to know and visit her over the past several years. But let me tell you something personal, I almost missed it. You see, after I baptized her, I wrote her a note that

she still keeps as a bookmark in her Bible. Here is a picture of what I said to her in that note.

Now what happened after I wrote this, is that I didn't visit her like I said I was going to for quite some time. When I finally got around to stopping by (which had been way too long), she said to me something along these lines: *"I began to think that you fibbed to me when you wrote that note."*

Ouch! I learned a valuable lesson that day. Not only do our *minutes matter,* but so do our *words.* How many times do we say things or have had things said to us and those words ring hollow. Sometimes we simply speak before we think. Since that first visit a few years back, I now try to stop and see Evelyn every week.

And to think, I almost missed it. As I sit and write this tonight, earlier today I stopped by for a visit and as I did, the thought hit me that I'm really going to miss the drive back this long, country road someday. Evelyn has Parkinson's and has her good and not so good days. I'm so glad that the Lord is continuing to teach me to number my days so that I may gain a heart of wisdom.

If you are a younger person reading this and the grey hairs seem so far away, please take this to heart. Actually, today I also had lunch with an eighteen-year-old graduate and in comparing our ages, he made the comment that went something like this, *"I'll never be that old."*

I told him I remember when my dad was forty-six and I was about nineteen that I looked at him and thought, *"He is so old, I'll never be that old."*

Now at fifty-one, my dad is seventy-eight and I look at him and say, *"Oh, it will be here sooner than I think."*

The things we learn as we get older. Oh, Lord, teach me to number my days.

Young people, enjoy life, but gain a heart of wisdom as fast as you can. I'm not referring to book knowledge, but wisdom that helps you look at life through a different lens. This can come only as you learn to walk close with the Lord and spend time in His Word. Church attendance and listening to good sermons are great. But nothing will train you to make your minutes matter more than spending time in God's Word. Actually, unless Jesus comes back before I die, these are the words I would like etched on my tombstone:

Kenneth Raymond Mele

November 13, 1966 – _____

"Stay in the Word"

Hebrews 4:11-12

May we also remember what James, the half-brother of Jesus wrote:

*"If anyone among you thinks he is religious, and does not bridle his tongue but deceives his own heart, this one's religion is useless. Pure and undefiled religion before God and the Father is this: to visit orphans and widows in their trouble, and to keep oneself unspotted from the world."*

—James 1:26-27

Now again, notice the entirety of this verse. It says in the last part that we should visit orphans and widows **and** keep ourselves unspotted from the world. The orphans and widows represent the forgotten ones. Take time for people that the world tends to forget about. They have so much to offer. And also keep yourself unspotted from the world's ways.

Make your *minutes matter.*

You will never regret giving time to the forgotten ones in the world and living righteously. However, we will regret if we simply consume all our time on ourselves and become selfish with our minutes.

So whatever we do, do it unto the Lord! May we ask Jesus at the start of each new day what He would have us to do with your minutes to truly make them matter in people's lives around us.

One day if we do, we will find ourselves standing before our Lord and hearing, *"Well done, well done!"*

And we won't say, *"Whatever!"*

We will simply say, *"I did it for You."*

## CHAPTER 6 - SMALL GROUP DISCUSSION

**Read Colossians 3.**

- How do these verses apply to my daily living and decision making?

How often do I find myself doing things for "man" rather than for Christ?

**Read Proverbs 16:31 and James 4:7.**

- How are these verse to be used and viewed in the right context?

Do my words and deeds line up with what the Lord would want me to do with my life?

**Read James 1:26-27.**

- What does it say pure religion is?
- Discuss the entirety of this verse and think about how you can apply these things to your life.

# CHAPTER 7

# Paying It Forward

I REMEMBER THE FIRST TIME someone used this phrase with me. My wife and I were at the Tampa Zoo on vacation and it was a really hot day! There was an *Icee* stand that looked really tempting, so we ordered one to bring us some relief from the heat. Well, it was in one of those nice plastic cups that you didn't want to throw away. I'm sure the cup cost much more than the flavored frozen water.

At the zoo.

So, when we finished it, I went and asked if we could get a refill. She filled it up again for us and I asked what I owed her and she said, *"don't worry about it, just pay it forward."*

Maybe you've had a similar experience when someone said this to you. If you were to look up the meaning of this phrase, Wikipedia defines it like this: *Pay it forward is an expression for describing of a good deed repaying it to others instead of to the original benefactor.*

I believe this phrase became popular because of a movie by the same name, but the idea of *paying it forward* goes back a long time.

Here is an example: You are driving on a road and about to come to a toll both that has a set fee of $2 per car. Every one passing through has to pay this fee. You also have to remember that this was before

*Easy Pass* where now we can slow down and simply pass through, and it deducts it from our account automatically.

You pay your $2, and then also pay the attendant $2 for the car directly behind you. If the person receiving that benefit from you wanted to *pay it forward*, they would then pay $2 for the car behind them . . . and so on, and so on.

I remember standing in line at McDonald's years ago, and there was a lady in front of me taking what seemed to be an exorbitant amount of time. When you're in line for fast food, guess what you would like? Fast food!

As I stood there waiting, gaining more impatient to order my own food, this lady finished what she was doing in front of me, and then turned around and began passing out $5 gift certificates to the people behind her in line. That day I really learned a lesson about patience and the idea of paying something forward and to think of others before yourself. I also realized not to assume you know what someone is up to before you know all the facts.

Could you imagine what this world would be like if we all lived doing unto others as we would want others to do unto us? Yes, living out the "golden rule" every day would change the world around us.

Paying something forward is easy to do when you are in line somewhere and want to bless someone behind you. A coffee shop, convenience store, a sporting event food stand . . . whatever! You name it, if you bless someone in any way, that gives them the opportunity to "pay it forward" to someone else.

Try it, you'll be amazed at people's reactions over something so little.

Now, this doesn't take place only when there is a price tag on something, but money does seem to speak the loudest for some reason. Money can be a dangerous trap if we grip it so tightly, and it's hard to release it out of our hands.

In this chapter, I would like to explore the idea and challenge us to make not only our *minutes matter*, but also our *money matter*. In reality, the key to making our money matter is to first realize the word "our" is the wrong choice of words. Ultimately, isn't it true that nothing we "*own*" is really ours? Let's look at a couple of verses.

**First, a word written by Moses in Deuteronomy 8:11-20:**

*"Beware that you do not forget the LORD your God by not keeping His commandments, His judgments, and His statutes which I commanded you today,*

*lest—when you have eaten and are full, and have built beautiful houses and dwell in them;*

*and when your herds and your flocks multiply, and your silver and your gold are multiplied, and all that you have is multiplied;*

*when your heart is lifted up, and you forget the LORD your God who brought you out of the land of Egypt, from the house of bondage;*

*who led you through that great and terrible wilderness, in which were fiery serpents and scorpions and thirsty land where there was no water; who brought water for you out of the flinty rock;*

*who fed you in the wilderness with manna, which your fathers did not know, that He might humble you and that He might test you, to do you good in the end–*

*then you say in your heart, 'My power and the might of my hand have gained me this wealth.'*

*And you shall remember the LORD your God, for it is He who gives you power to get wealth, that He may establish His covenant which He swore to your fathers, as it is this day.*

*Then it shall be, if you by any means forget the LORD your God, and follow other gods, and serve them and worship them, I testify against you this day that you shall surely perish.*

*As the nations which the LORD destroys before you, so you shall perish, because you would not be obedient to the voice of the LORD your God."*

**Then a word from the Apostle Paul found in 1 Timothy 6:7:**

*"For we brought nothing into this world, and it is certain we can carry nothing out."*

This is great advice that Paul gave to young Timothy.

Nada, zip, zilch . . . nothing! So why is it that we hold onto our stuff so much?

Have you ever seen this at a funeral?

Now that would be funny, right? This picture makes me laugh, but it so challenges my heart as well! We know we would never see this, but so many live this way maybe without realizing it.

It makes me ask the question myself, *"What am I living for? Am I making His money matter that He has allowed me to be a steward over?"*

I thought about this more recently as I was writing checks and paying bills one day. I have to do this every couple of weeks. Do I get excited about writing my checks out for taxes, the mortgage, the cell phone or water authority? How about the electric company, now that really gets me excited!

No, the only checks I get really excited about writing are the ones I make out for furthering God's Kingdom and doing His work. Now when my wife and I give to different ministries or missionaries . . . that gets us excited! When we give to the Lord's work here on earth and invest in expanding God's Kingdom, what you're really doing is paying it forward.

Luke shares a story that is found only in his Gospel. Neither Matthew, Mark, nor John record this parable.

*"Then one from the crowd said to Him, 'Teacher, tell my brother to divide the inheritance with me.'*

*But He said to him, 'Man, who made Me a judge or an arbitrator over you?'*

*And He said to them, 'Take heed and beware of covetousness, for one's life does not consist in the abundance of the things he possesses.'*

*Then He spoke a parable to them, saying: 'The ground of a certain rich man yielded plentifully.*

*And he thought within himself, saying, 'What shall I do, since I have no room to store my crops?'*

*So he said, 'I will do this: I will pull down my barns and build greater, and there I will store all my crops and my goods.*

*And I will say to my soul, 'Soul, you have many goods laid up for many years; take your ease; eat, drink, and be merry.'*

*But God said to him, 'Fool! This night your soul will be required of you; then whose will those things be which you have provided?'*

*'So is he who lays up treasure for himself, and is not rich toward God.'"*

—Luke 12:13-21

I'll share the last verse of this story at the end this chapter. But doesn't this remind you of the storage units that we have seen pop up in America over the past several decades?

Now I must say that at times they do serve a purpose if you are in between moves or are storing something that will be used in the near future. But I believe the majority of storage units in this country are full of stuff that could no longer fit in our homes, garages, attics, basements, or sheds. So, instead of giving it away to maybe those in need or even downsizing the way we live, we decide to "build a bigger barn" and even pay for it to hold all our stuff.

I discovered something very valuable when we were building a new home and had to store furniture and other items in one of these units until our house was complete. The one thing that I realized and the Holy Spirit made me aware of was how much of what I had stored there I could really live without. I didn't even miss those things. When it comes right down to it, we really can live on very little. So why do we have so much?

The Lord is still working on me with this and at times I still have to ask for His forgiveness for the abundance of possessions I can easily accumulate . . . even if it was a great deal! One thing that helped shed a light on this even more was when we downsized from that home we built to the one we currently live in. To get rid of stuff as we took up residence in a smaller home felt so good!

The question we must all seriously ask ourselves is this: *"will our possessions speak for or against us someday?"*

So, what was Jesus saying in this story? Let's take a look at this last verse in this parable that should really cause us to stop and *take heed.*

*"And He said to them, 'Take heed and beware of covetousness, for one's life does not consist in the abundance of the things he possesses.'"*

Lord, please help us to give it away before we die with so much! As Job said, *"naked I came from my mother's womb, And naked shall I return there."*

They may dress us up in our favorite suit or dress when we die, but underneath those clothes, we all leave the same way, cold and buck naked!

Let's begin to "pay it forward."

## CHAPTER 7 - SMALL GROUP DISCUSSION

**Read Deuteronomy 8:11-20.**

- Why do you think the increase in their lives caused them to forget the Lord?
- How can we prevent this from happening in our own lives?

**Read 1 Timothy 6:7 and Luke 12:12-21.**

- Do you see how these can relate to our lives and the world we live in today? If so, how?

Take a personal inventory of your possessions.

- Ask yourself, "Will they speak for or against me someday?"
- If against me, what changes must I make in this area of my life?

# Treasure Hunt

THIS CHAPTER WILL EXPAND A little further as a continuation from the previous one. In the Sermon on the Mount, Jesus made a statement that should really catch our attention. It is located right after He teaches the disciples how to pray, how to give, and also how to fast.

Here's what Jesus said:

> "Do not lay up for yourselves treasure on earth, where moth and rust destroy and where thieves break in and steal;
>
> but lay up for yourselves treasure in heaven, where neither moth nor rust destroys and where thieves do not break in and steal.
>
> For where your treasure is, there your heart will be also."
>
> —Matthew 6:19-21

Where your treasure is, there your heart will be also?

Okay, so the question we need to really be asking ourselves is this, *"Where's my treasure?"*

Why? Because that's what our heart beats for the most. So let's go on a treasure hunt!

Do you remember when you were a kid, did you ever pretend as if you were hunting for hidden treasure? Maybe you were a pirate searching for that treasure chest of gold. Sometimes it took a while. It took time, energy, creative thinking, and effort. But as kids, we had fun with it and used what sometimes we lose as adults, our imagination. Finding the treasure was not always easy.

In reality though, finding earthly treasure may not be easy either, but so many chase after it. The desire for more earthly treasure consumes people, when in fact, all this earthly treasure will eventually be destroyed when we finally kiss this earth goodbye.

I like to look at our time here on earth as a vacation. This earth is not our home, we are simply on a vacation and someday very soon if we are believers and followers of Jesus, we'll be home with Him forever! You may be saying to yourself, *"yeah, right, very soon. I've been hearing that since I was a kid, that Jesus is coming back."* His time table and ours are two very different things.

In Psalm 90:10a, Moses says something very interesting:
*"The days of our lives are seventy years; And if by reason of strength they are eighty years."*

People in Moses' day lived well beyond seventy or eighty, right? Adam lived to be 930, his sons Seth and Lamech were 912 and 777, Noah was 950, and good ol' Methuselah, the oldest man to ever walk the earth, was 969. Even Abraham lived to be 175.

And Moses, well, 120. Now, I won't go into why people lived so long, I'll leave that book for the theologians. But I do find it very interesting that Moses chose (or I should say God inspired him to write) *"seventy . . . and if by reason of strength they are eighty."*

According to the *World Health Organization*, the average life expectancy of the global population in 2015 was 71.4. Do you think when Moses wrote this that the people were thinking, *"What are you talking about Moses? You're even well over 100 yourself."*

But I believe the Lord God Almighty was inspiring Moses to prophesy for us today and say, *"seventy . . . maybe eighty."* Yes, some live longer, some die younger. But worldwide, the average was 71.4 in 2015.

If you live to be 71.4, that would seem like a good many number years and lots of minutes to make matter. But actually today, that seems young to me as I just turned fifty, and my parents are in their mid to late seventies. But say you are 71.5 years.

Let's take a look at what Peter wrote in 2 Peter 3:8:

*"But, beloved, do not forget this one thing, that with the Lord one*
*day is as a thousand years, and a thousand years as one day."*

So, in our minds, 71.5 seems like a good age and many years. But in reality, as you get older, isn't it true that our years seem to fly by?

I heard someone say recently, *"Why is it that years seem to fly but days seem to go slow?"*

Can anyone relate out there? As I work on this chapter, I just had a college student stop in my office to say *"hi."*

As we were talking, he was sharing his schedule with me. He is a freshman at Penn State. I told him to enjoy these four years and gave him the advice that my Uncle Carl gave to me when I began my college career in 1984.

He said, *"Enjoy these four years, they will be some of the greatest years of your life and they will go by so quickly."*

This young man looked at me and said, *"Really, but these first four days seemed to take forever."*

I said to him as he stood there, *"Wow, I was just writing about this and it would be a perfect example."*

He said, *"Oh, wow, maybe I'll be in a book?"*

I said, *"Maybe."* So there you go, Eric.


So to put this in perspective, let's compute out what years look like in the Lord's mind compared to our human understanding according to what Peter said above.

1,000 years equals one day (with the Lord). This means that if (in the Lord's mind) we were to live to the age of 1,000, it would be the equivalent of one day to the Lord, a mere twenty-four hours. Now, we know that nobody will live to be 1,000 years old. So let's go with an age that my wife and I just turned so that the numbers work out evenly, fifty. If you are fifty years old, that breaks down to (in the Lord's mind), one hour and twenty minutes. In His mind, my wife and I have been plodding around on this earth for about an hour and a half. Crazy, huh? Even Methuselah, when he took his last breathe at 969, almost lived one whole day on this earth from heaven's perspective, and then the Lord called him home. So, by doing the math, you can see that every ten years of your life here on earth is equivalent to about sixteen minutes in heaven. Read that last line again.

This next verse at times makes my brain hurt from trying to figure it out. Especially when I combine it with what I was just sharing, and I'm not quite sure I can completely grasp its meaning. But one day we will see clearly because it tells us in 1 Corinthians 13:12 that *"now we see in a mirror, dimly, but then face to face. Now I know in part, but then I shall know just as I also am known."*

Here's the verse that sends me thinking.

*"Before I formed you in the womb I knew you . . . "*

—Jeremiah 1:5

**Before**? Now, I know that everyone reading this already knows this, but we had to be conceived first before we became present in the womb of our mother. But this verse says that even **before** we were conceived in the womb, God already knew us.

Could this mean that we were, in some way, with the Lord and in His presence before we were in the womb? It may not have been physically, and I don't want to get weird here, but it does say <u>He knew us</u>.

Could this mean that when God chose us to be conceived in our mother's womb, that at that moment we somehow left His presence and were conceived? So, if that be the case, I've been gone from the Lord's presence for about an hour and twenty minutes from when He began to knit me together in my mother's womb. And one day when I return to Him, He will say, *"Welcome home . . . it hasn't even been that long."*

Obviously, I can't say this is exactly how it's going to play out, but it sure does get your mind thinking, does it not? I'm just glad He knows my name, how about you?

Why not take a break and turn to Psalm 139 in your Bible. This is my daughter's favorite chapter in God's Word, and for good reason.

Here are some thoughts from this chapter:

*"Such knowledge is too wonderful for me; It is high, I cannot attain it."* (verse 6)

*"For you formed my inward parts; You covered me in my mother's womb."* (verse 13)

*"Your eyes saw my substance, being yet unformed. And in your book they all were written, The days fashioned for me, When as yet there were none of them."* (verse 16)

If we are given only such a short time here on earth, why do we chase after the treasure of this earth with so much vigor rather than spending our time, effort, resources, and energy building treasure that will last forever? That is the million dollar question. Solomon referred to this as a "chasing after the wind."

The reason that building up our treasure in heaven is so difficult is because it comes with no earthly reward. Actually, if we seek to be recognized here on earth, we lose our reward in heaven. Jesus reminds us of this a little earlier, again, from His famous Sermon on the Mount:

*"Take heed that you do not do your charitable deeds before men, to be seen by them. Otherwise you have no reward from your Father in heaven.*

*Therefore, when you do a charitable deed, do not sound a trumpet before you as the hypocrites do in the synagogues and in the streets, that they may have glory from men. Assuredly, I say to you, they have their reward.*

*But when you do a charitable deed, do not let your left hand know what your right hand is doing,*

*that your charitable deed may be in secret; and your Father who sees in secret will Himself reward you openly."*

—Matthew 6:1-4

Why is it when it comes to getting a reward that so often we will take the recognition now and forfeit the eternal reward later? Let us begin to search for that eternal reward and not even worry about the earthly stuff that only makes us chase after the wrong things and those hollow rewards. Actually, in this passage you just read, did you notice that they were *"doing good things?"*

We can do good things or accumulate earthly wealth and at the same time have no reward waiting for us in heaven. May we truly learn to seek the eternal treasure that provides absolutely no reward here on earth, but great reward once we are with the Lord. May we work towards building up the *silver, gold, and precious stone* rather than wasting our time on *wood, hay, and straw.*

May we not forget what the Apostle Paul wrote to the church in Corinth.

> *"Now if anyone builds on this foundation with gold, silver, precious stones, wood, hay, straw,*
>
> *each one's work will become clear; for the Day will declare it, because it will be revealed by fire; and the fire will test each one's work, of what sort it is.*
>
> *If anyone's work which he has built on it endures, he will receive a reward.*
>
> *If anyone's work is burned, he will suffer loss; but he himself will be saved, yet so as through fire."*
>
> —1 Corinthians 3:12-15

When we come to believe and follow Jesus Christ, He is our foundation that we then begin to build upon. Notice, Paul writes, *"**If** anyone builds on this foundation . . . "*

Before going further as we come towards the end of this book, may I ask *if* you have begun to do this? If is such a "big" word, and if you have not decided to build your life on Christ, you're on shaky ground. Actually, Jesus calls it sinking sand.

Every human being has a choice to make of what they build their life upon, and no one can make that choice for them. Sure, when children are young, mom and dad choose for them, but as they begin life on their own, no longer is the choice their parents, they now become accountable and responsible for their own foundation: Solid Rock versus Sinking Sand.

What's your choice?

The great thing if you have not chosen to believe and follow Jesus Christ with your life is that your heart is still beating because you are reading this book. But none of us know when that last beat may be. It could be even before you finish this chapter.

Before saying *yes* or *no* to Jesus, the Bible tells us to count the cost. Following Jesus demands everything.

Here is something Jesus said that we must consider before we say *yes* to become true followers of Jesus Christ.

> *"Now great multitudes went with Him. And he turned and said to them,*
>
> *'If anyone comes to Me and does not hate his father and mother, wife and children, brothers and sisters, yes, and his own life also, he cannot be My disciple.*
>
> *And whoever does not bear his cross and come after Me cannot be My disciple.*
>
> *For which of you, intending to build a tower, does not sit down first and count the cost, whether he has enough to finish it–*
>
> *lest, after he has laid the foundation, and is not able to finish, all who see it begin to mock him,*
>
> *saying 'This man began to build and was not able to finish.'*
>
> *Or what king, going to make war against another king, does not sit down first and consider whether he is able with ten thousand to meet him who comes against him with twenty thousand?*
>
> *Or else, while the other is still a great way off, he sends a delegation and asks conditions of peace.*

*So likewise, whoever of you does not forsake all that he has cannot
be My disciple."'*

—Luke 14:25-33

This may seem radical, but following Jesus means forsaking all.
When we choose to follow Christ and go on this *treasure hunt* for
eternity, we need to take it seriously. To my understanding, *hating
one's family* means to *desire something less than something else.* In other
words, Jesus Christ must become first above everything and everyone
else in our lives.

Why did Jesus state it like this? Well, in His day, when you decided
to follow Him, you were putting your very closest relationships on the
line. The pain of rejection and persecution was felt from the closest
of family members. Today, in some parts of our world this still happens. Some die for the sake of becoming a true disciple and follower
of Christ.

I believe Jesus was saying, *"Are you really ready for this?"*

If so, it's a journey that won't be easy, but one you will never
regret. Yes, there will be times of trouble, pain, and adversity, but as
you build on His foundation, you will stand because you're building
on the Solid Rock.

Trouble, pain, and adversity comes to everyone, those who follow
Jesus and those who don't. What's the difference? It's whether you
stand or sink.

Back to the Sermon on the Mount.

> *"Therefore whoever hears these sayings of Mine, and does them, I
> will liken to a wise man who built his house on the rock;*
> *and the rain descended, the floods came, and the winds blew and
> beat on that house; and it did not fall, for it was founded on the rock.*
> *But everyone who hears these sayings of Mine, and does not do
> them, will be like a foolish man who built his house on the sand;*

*and the rain descended, the floods came, and the winds blew and*
*beat on that house, and it fell. And great was its fall."*
—Matthew 7:24-27

So, where do we begin? As I sit and write this part of the book, the calendar has turned over to December, and we are into the Christmas season. There is a verse in the Gospel of Luke that describes just who Jesus is and what part He wants to have in our lives if we are to forsake all else and follow Him.

Here it is:

*"For there is born to you this day in the city of David a Savior, who*
*is Christ the Lord."*
—Luke 2:11

As we read the accounts of the birth of Christ from Luke and Matthew's Gospel, we see that Jesus came to save us from our sins.

*"And she will bring forth a Son, and you shall call His name JESUS,*
*for He will save His people from their sins."*
—Matthew 1:21

I'm so glad that Jesus is my Savior, because boy did I need my sins forgiven and covered by His blood! How many of you can relate?

But Jesus desires us to experience more than even that, as great as that is. If you look back at that verse in Luke and break that verse apart, it explains who our Savior is . . . *"who is Christ the Lord."*

Jesus came to be our Savior and forgive us of our sins, but He also desires and needs to become Lord of our lives. These two words, Savior and Lord, go hand in hand. You cannot have one without the other. But how many try to pray a prayer to have their sins forgiven and make sure they're going to heaven, but never make Christ the Lord of their lives?

Usually two things happen when people do this. One, they never grow or are very sporadic in their worship, their giving, and serving. Or two, they fall away and you never see them again after a short season.

Most likely, there is a possibility that they were never saved in the first place because they truly never counted the cost.

We cannot ask Jesus to forgive us but not be Lord over our lives. Jesus wants every part of us. Not only to *come and live in our heart,* but for Him to *rule and reign over our lives as Lord.* Our relationships, our habits, our finances, our professions, our talents, our time, our thoughts, and our minutes. Every part of us must become radically and completely surrendered to the lordship of Christ. That's why Jesus said before you choose to follow Him, "count the cost."

So what does *Lord* actually mean? The Greek word for Lord that is used in a verse I will share below is *kyrios.* This word means to have power, dominion, authority, and the right to master. Wow! So, Jesus wants to have power, dominion, and authority over my life and desires to be my master? Well, yes. But not in a bad way as a slave.

No, He desires to control our lives with an overwhelming amount of His love, not by force. Jesus doesn't make us do anything, rather, when our lives our fully submitted to His authority, His all-encompassing love begins to saturate every fiber of our being, and we begin to function with freedom and power under the direction of the Holy Spirit.

If you want to do an interesting study with your Bible sometime, do this. Get two different color highlighters. Begin in the New Testament and read from Matthew to Revelation. In one color, highlight every time you see the word "Savior" used. In the second color, highlight the word "Lord."

I have yet to do this myself, but I read in my study Bible that the word *Savior* is used 16 times in the New Testament, the word *Lord* over 450 times!

Why? Because Jesus cannot just be your Savior, He must become your Lord. I also read where the creed of the New Testament church was "Jesus is Lord," not "Jesus is Savior."

Even at the communion table, you have heard these verses read from 1 Corinthians 11:23-29. Notice how many times the word, *Lord,* is used:

*"For I received from the Lord that which I also delivered to you: that the Lord Jesus on the same night in which He was betrayed took bread;*

*and when He had given thanks, He broke it and said, 'Take, eat; this is My body which is broken for you; do this in remembrance of Me.'*

*In the same manner He also took the cup after supper, saying, 'This cup is the new covenant in My blood. This do, as often as you drink it, in remembrance of Me.'*

*For as often as you eat this bread and drink this cup, you proclaim the Lord's death till He comes.*

*Therefore whoever eats this bread or drinks this cup of the Lord in an unworthy manner will be guilty of the body and blood of the Lord.*

*But let a man examine himself, and so let him eat of the bread and drink of the cup.*

*For he who eats and drinks in an unworthy manner eats and drinks judgment to himself, not discerning the Lord's body.*

*For this reason many are weak and sick among you, and many sleep.*

*For if we would judge ourselves, we would not be judged.*

*But when we are judged, we are chastened by the Lord, that we may not be condemned with the world."*

WOW!

When we come to the table, we are drinking the cup of the **Lord.** He gave His all and so must we. We must be careful not to come to this table with areas of our lives not submitted to Christ as Lord.

Aren't you glad that it says to examine ourselves so that we don't come under judgment? What grace and love is found at the communion table as Christ gives us the opportunity to examine and judge ourselves before receiving. We must be careful to do so, and once we do, we are free to receive. Lord, You are so good to us!

*"That if you confess with your mouth the Lord Jesus and believe in your heart that God raised Him from the dead, you will be saved. For 'whoever calls on the name of the LORD shall be saved.'"*
—Romans 10:9,13

If you have never surrendered your life to Jesus as Lord and Savior, here might be a good place to start from the depths of your heart in prayer.

"Lord Jesus, I need You so much . . . I realize how much I've sinned against You . . . that You came and gave Your life for me . . . shed Your blood and took my sin to the cross . . . You gave everything You have for me. And right now, I choose to count the cost and surrender my life to You and follow You . . . First, forgive me and cleanse me of my sin with Your blood You shed for my life . . . I give You my life, every part of me, and I accept You as not only my Savior, but also as Lord over every area of my life . . . Thank You for dying for me, so that I may live completely surrendered for You!"

If you are praying that prayer for the first time, congratulations! I would love to hear from you and help you pursue Christ and share some vital next steps in your life. If you are already following Christ, may we continue to battle and fight what the Apostle Paul calls the *good fight of faith*. It's so worth the battle!

## CHAPTER 8 - SMALL GROUP DISCUSSION

**Read Matthew 6:19-21.**

- What does, *"for where your treasure is, there your heart will be also"* mean?

**Read Psalm 90:10.**

- Depending on your age, how does this make you feel?

Compare 2 Peter 3:8 with Jeremiah 1:5

- What thoughts come to mind when you read these together?

**Read Psalm 139:6, 13, 16.**

- How do these verses make you feel about the Lord creating you?

**Read 1 Corinthians 3:12-15.**

- Ask yourself, is my work *"silver, gold, and precious stone"* or more *"wood, hay, and stubble?"*

**Read Luke 14:25-33.**

- Have you ever really counted the cost of following Jesus? If not, why not take time to do so right now.
- Have you ever prayed to ask Christ to be both your Savior and Lord of your life? How should this look in my life as I live that out?

# Where Are You?

DO YOU EVER FEEL LIKE you've wasted something? One thing that is a pet peeve of mine is the amount of food we waste in our country. I heard recently that the amount of food Americans throw away could wipe out hunger around the world. But not only food, how many minutes, which turn into hours, then days and years are wasted on things that really don't matter in the long run? As I wrote earlier in the book, this is not so much a *time management* book as it is a *heart management* book.

The one thing that we don't want to say we wasted at the end of our lives are the beats of our hearts. And each and every one of them is a gift from the Lord God Almighty, the Giver of life!

Here are some staggering statistics that I read from a study done by MSN in an article entitled, "30 Surprising facts about how we spend our time."[6] These are based on the average lifespan of seventy-five. As you read these numbers, keep in mind the number of days that you would exercise over fifty years of your life at 180 minutes a week. That number would be less than one year, 325 days.

- Twenty-six years of your life are spent sleeping (one third of your life, but time well spent).
- Eleven years will be spent watching TV.
- Eight years will be spent shopping.
- Three years washing clothes.

- We spend only six minutes laughing every day, which translates into 115 days over a lifetime. A generation earlier (1950s) chuckled eighteen minutes a day! At least that came out to 345 days of laughter.
- Seven years is spent lying awake (my wife would probably say, *"double that"*).
- Only twenty-seven days are spent being romantic with each other (sad statistic for marriages today).
- Five months complaining.
- 10.3 years spent working if you put in forty hours per week between the ages of twenty to sixty-five. Note, more time is spent watching television.
- A child born in 2013 will have spent one entire year in front of a screen by the time they turn seven.
- One in three teenagers send more than 100 text messages a day.
- 38,003 hours, or nearly 4.4 years of your life, is spent eating.
- Five years surfing the internet. How many days spent exercising? Not quite one year.
- Women will spend 14,000 hours, or 1.5 years, brushing, washing, blow-drying, straightening, curling, or cutting their hair.
- People check their phone every six and a half minutes, which translates into 150 times during sixteen waking hours.
- Americans spend ninety-three percent of their lives indoors, either in a building or a car.

Now take a look at another article I read entitled, "8 Things Successful People Never Waste Time Doing."[7]

Productive, successful people . . .

- Don't get sucked into social media.
- Don't go throughout the day without a plan.
- Don't do emotionally draining activities.
- Don't worry about things they can't control.

- Don't hang out with negative people.
- Don't dwell on past mistakes.
- Don't focus on what other people are doing.
- Don't put themselves last in priority.

You see, if we aren't healthy, we can't be healthy for those around us. It's like when you are on a plane and the stewardess goes over the procedures concerning safety if there is an emergency. When they explain the oxygen mask falling from the ceiling, they remind you to put it on yourself first. Then, after you have done so, you will have strength to help others around you. We must be healthy ourselves so that we can effectively help others around us who are hurting or in need.

Before going any further, check out this verse concerning that muscle that pumps blood throughout our bodies and without it our days would be over.

*"Keep your heart with all diligence, For out of it spring the is-sues of life."*

—Proverbs 4:23

Diligence, all diligence. Diligence is defined by some as *determination and careful effort.* Another definition I came across said that it is *earnest and persistent application to an undertaking; steady effort.*

Apply this to the verse above and we can see how we are to persistently work at protecting our hearts. For this is where life begins and ends. Waste the beats of our heart and so much comes to a screeching halt!

We may not die physically, but our purpose for living can become meaningless if we waste the beats of our heart. It reminds me of the conversation that took place in the Garden of Eden back in Genesis:

*"And the woman said to the serpent, 'We may eat the fruit of the trees of the garden;*
*but of the fruit of the tree which is in the midst of the garden, God said, 'You shall not eat it, nor shall you touch it, lest you die.'"*

*Then the serpent said to the woman, 'You will not surely die.*
*For God knows that in the day you eat of it your eyes will be opened,*
*and you will be like God, knowing good and evil.'"*

—Genesis 3:2-5

Now before I go further, you have to realize how much I love to have fun. Ask my wife, she would often say when the kids were growing up, *"I don't have two kids, I have three!"*

Actually, I believe that kicking back and having fun is part of not wasting the beats of your heart because it says in Proverbs 17:22 that *"a merry heart does good, like medicine."* Sometimes we need to stop being so serious and simply laugh, even at ourselves. We are pretty funny people, you know? So laughter and fun is good!

When it comes to wasting beats of our heart, it really boils down to doing things in excess that when looked at through the lens of Christ are meaningless. Do you remember years ago when the acronym *WWJD* became popular?

It really began to get people thinking about acting like Jesus. People would find themselves in a certain situation and stop and ask themselves, *"What would Jesus do?"*

Isn't that the ultimate goal, to be more like Jesus? When I'm challenged by the Holy Spirit inside of me about certain things, I will try to pause and ask myself that question. I may not say those words exactly, but the thought is there. When I sit down in front of the television, after a time, I hear Him saying, *"That's enough."*

When I surf the web or get on Facebook and I get to the point where I hear His voice say, *"K.R., let's move on to something else,"* I have a choice to make. This can even happen with things that may be good. When you are working hard, but you know you've worked more hours over the past few days as your family is home waiting for you, you have a choice to put down the work and go home or continue grinding away.

Hey, it will be there tomorrow. Believe me, your kids won't. Just a few months ago, I walked my daughter down the aisle to be married and I asked myself, *"Where did those twenty-one years just go?"*

No, we won't die physically by wasting beats, but something will be lost as we let these beats skip by doing meaningless things. We will lose God's purpose for living, and that we can't afford to forfeit. Unless we THINK like Jesus, we're not going to act like Jesus. To begin to do what Jesus would do, we must first begin to say *WWJT.*

We must learn to discipline our minds because it reminds us in 2 Corinthians 10:5 to bring every thought into captivity to the obedience of Christ. When our minds begin to think like Christ, our ways will become like Christ.

Let's ask ourselves first, *"What would Jesus think."*

Let's continue with this deceitful conversation from Genesis.

> *"So when the woman saw that the tree was good for food, that it was pleasant to the eyes, and a tree desirable to make one wise, she took of its fruit and ate. She also gave to her husband with her, and he ate.*
>
> *Then the eyes of both of them were opened, and they knew that they were naked; and they sewed fig leaves together and made themselves coverings."*
>
> —Genesis 3:6-7

What Eve was convinced of by Satan (the god of this age), and also Adam because if you notice, he was *with her,* was that they were missing out on something better than what they already had. Our world (and the god of this age) today is still trying to lure us away with so many devices and here is the lie that Satan is still trying to feed us, *"you're missing out on something better than you already have."*

Adam and Eve were the only ones to ever know what it was like to have a pure, holy, undefiled relationship with God. The only man and woman to ever experience only love, no pain, no sorrow, no conviction of sin . . . until they bit! Satan is still the master deceiver and is still trying to get us to bite. It's what he does best.

Here is what Jesus had to say about our adversary in the Gospel of John:

> *"You are of your father the devil, and the desires of your father you want to do. He was a murderer from the beginning, and does not stand in the truth, because there is no truth in him. When he speaks a lie, he speaks from his own resources, for he is a liar and the father of it."*
>
> —John 8:44

Satan is still trying to get us to bite. He is trying to say to all believers, *"what you have with Jesus, well, that's okay, but I have something better."*

He wants to deceive us into believing that our time can be better utilized if we think more about ourselves and what we want rather than what the Lord wants to do with our lives. He speaks lies, but he does it so good and makes it sound so appealing, like it will benefit us if we give into the bait he throws our way, hoping we will take it hook, line, and sinker. In other words, well, in his words, he says, *"you won't surely die . . . you will be like God."*

Sounds pretty good, huh? But immediately after that first bite, Adam and Eve looked at each other and were ashamed of their nakedness. They were guilt-ridden, and rather than becoming like God, they ran from Him and were afraid to face Him. They thought they were going to become like God and in reality they became the opposite of Him.

Then something interesting happened. As they were hiding, God came looking for them. He knew exactly where Adam and Eve were. But He asked a question, actually the first recorded question ever asked in the Bible, *"Where are you?"*

> *"And they heard the sound of the LORD God walking in the garden in the cool of the day, and Adam and his wife hid themselves from the presence of the LORD God among the trees of the garden.*
>
> *Then the LORD God called to Adam and said to him, "Where are you?"*
>
> —Genesis 3:8-9

Let me pause here and point out a couple of things. Notice that the name is no longer simply *God*, but now it is *Lord God*. With this new word, *Lord*, God now became a personal God to Adam and Eve, not just the God who created the heavens and the earth, but now also *Yahweh* (Jehovah), a God who was now in a personal relationship with His children.

God, now the Lord God, was looking for His kids. And may I add, after they disobeyed Him. I would not have wanted to be in their fig leaves. He asks Adam the question, *"Where are you?"*

> *"Then the LORD God took the man and put him in the garden of Eden to tend and keep it.*
>
> *And the LORD God commanded the man, saying, 'Of every tree of the garden you may freely eat;*
>
> *but of the tree of knowledge of good and evil you shall not eat, for in the day that you eat of it you shall surely die.'"*
>
> —Genesis 2:15-17

Here is a question you may have never thought of and answered. Where was Eve when the Lord God gave this command to Adam that you just read? She was just a thought in God's mind, she was not even created yet. Here is the next verse in the story . . .

> *"And the LORD God said, 'It is not good that man should be alone; I will make him a helper comparable to him.'"*
>
> —Genesis 2:18

When the Lord God gave the command to Adam not to eat, Eve was not even created yet. No wonder He came looking for Adam. It seems Adam told Eve about not eating from that tree because of the conversation she had with the serpent, but still, this was first on Adam's shoulders, and then Eve's.

Imagine the scene in the garden when He finds Adam and Eve with coverings over their naked bodies and asks, *"Where are you?"*

Did God really mean, physically, *where are you*?

God already knew that. And right after God asks this question we see Adam's reply:

> So he said, "I heard Your voice in the garden, and I was afraid because I was naked; and I hid myself."
>
> —Genesis 3:10

The question God asked Adam wanted to reveal the heart of the matter, not their physical location. I find it interesting that Adam uses the pronoun, I rather than we.

"I heard . . . I was afraid . . . I was naked . . . I hid myself."

Then, something happens where blame begins to be tossed around like my grandma used to toss around a big bowl of spaghetti.

> "And He said, 'Who told you that you were naked? Have you eaten from the tree of which I commanded you that you should not eat?'
>
> Then the man said, 'The woman whom You gave to be with me, she gave me of the tree, and I ate.'
>
> And the LORD God said to the woman, 'What is this you have done?' The woman said, 'The serpent deceived me, and I ate.'"
>
> —Genesis 3:11-13

Adam blamed Eve, Eve blamed the serpent, but in reality, Adam really blamed God. Did you notice before he blamed Eve he said, "The woman <u>whom You gave</u> to be with me."

The first thing we must do when we want to get the heart beating in the right rhythm is to accept responsibility of where we are. Not physically, but spiritually. So ask yourself this question, "where am I?"

The life of David should be a consolation to all of us. Because as much as he messed up, he was still called a man after God's own heart. That should be comforting to each and every one of us. Oh, but the grace of God!

I love the fact that when God came searching for Adam and Eve, when He asked them the questions He did, it says He did so as the Lord God. He didn't revert back to just God, but maintained His personal name towards them, His children.

Years ago, probably in my thirties, I remember my heart was physically skipping beats. When it did so, I could actually feel it in my chest,
and it would take my breath away for a moment. I would sit or lay
down, and usually it would last only a short time, and it was back to
beating normal again. It was a weird feeling, and I knew something
wasn't quite right.

The Lord God has created us and wants our hearts to beat normally
for His purposes. But, unfortunately we have an enemy who is lying
to us all and trying his hardest to get our hearts off beat. Satan is trying to get them off beat so that we waste them and don't use them to
further God's kingdom.

When our hearts beat after the wrong things, it will eventually
catch up to us and eventually feel like we are dying spiritually. Oh,
you won't feel that way immediately because another trick of Satan's
is that he makes sin have pleasure in it; but as it says in the Word, that
pleasure lasts only for a season and ends in destruction.

Look what it says about Moses in Hebrews 11:25-26, *"choosing rather
to suffer affliction with the people of God than to enjoy the passing pleasures
of sin, esteeming the reproach of Christ greater riches than the treasures in
Egypt; for he looked to the reward."*

If (there's that two letter big word again) your sin feels good, that's
no surprise. But it's a trick because eventually it will destroy you if
you continually bite at that bait.

And the fact is, we know it's not right, just like my heart skipping
a beat wasn't correct either. You know, and I know, what we are doing
with our beats.

*"Where are you . . . where am I?"*

As we evaluate our hearts, let's make it a goal to guard our hearts,
because it truly is where life springs from! We must make sure our
hearts are beating in the right rhythm if we're truly going to make
our minutes matter.

## CHAPTER 9 - SMALL GROUP DISCUSSION

In reviewing the amount of time we spend on things, what would you say you "waste the most time on?"

**Read Proverbs 4:23.**

- How well would you say you're doing at *"keeping your heart with all diligence?"*

**Read 2 Corinthians 10:5.**

- How do we begin to change our thinking to make it more like Christ?

Adam blamed Eve, Eve blamed the serpent, but ultimately Adam really blamed God. How important is it to take personal responsibility with our actions or inactions?

- Would you agree that it is impossible to grow until we do so? Why or why not?

Are there some "pleasures of sin" that you are enjoying that could eventually lead to destructions that you must rid yourself of?

# What Is Your Life?

WOW, 1986! SOME THINGS TO remember about 1986:

- First class stamp—22 cents
- Gallon of gas—93 cents (sometimes I remember paying 69 or 79 cents during "gas wars")
- Dozen eggs—87 cents
- Gallon of milk—$2.22
- Average cost of a new house—$89,430
- Best-selling Christmas toy in 1986—Lazer Tag (1983's was the Cabbage Patch Kids)

Do you realize how quickly thirty years has slipped by? 1986 changed the trajectory of our family forever. My mom and dad's marriage, which had struggled over the first 25 years was saved, only by them giving their lives to Christ and beginning to follow Him wholeheartedly. That's another story, but I'm so thankful that my mom and dad didn't become another statistic.

I had just begun my last two years of college at the main campus of Penn State University. After my mom and dad came to Christ, they desperately wanted me to as well but at the time I was having too much fun, or so I thought, and didn't have time for Jesus. But I watched their lives change, and that probably more than anything became a testimony for me. Is there any greater testimony that we can have than a changed life by the power of the Holy Spirit?

I love the verse found in 2 Corinthians 5:17:

*"Therefore, if anyone is in Christ, he is a new creation; old things*
*have passed away; behold, all things have become new."*

A year later, I met my wife-to-be. We grew up about twenty minutes from each other just northeast of the great city of champions,
Pittsburgh, Pennsylvania. But we went to different high schools and
never knew each other until that wonderful summer of 1987.

The minute I laid eyes on her, I wanted to take her out on a date.
Well, at the time I asked her, she told me she "kind of had a boyfriend."
Now, I don't know about you, but in my mind "kind of" was like a wide
open invitation for a date. So I asked if I could pick her up and go to
the Monroeville Mall.

Hey, shopping at the mall wasn't really a date, was it? The next
day I decided to send her a dozen roses at work. That night she made
her way home from work with her roses in hand and her boyfriend
was on the porch waiting for her.

He saw the roses in her arms and said, *"Oh that's nice, you got flowers*
*for your dad."*

Gina said, *"They're not for my dad."*

He then said, *"Oh, for your mom?"*

Gina responded, *"No."*

Then he said, *"Uh-oh."*

And Gina looked at him and said, *"Yes."*

Fast forward six weeks later, and I was down on one knee asking
her to marry me. I was not about to let this one slip by. Gina has been
an amazing wife for almost thirty years now, and I could not have
imagined travelling this road without her.

Whether she realizes it or not, she has not wasted the beats of her
heart and her family is a testament to that. She seems to always be
thinking about the other person and putting their needs before her
own. A word that helps describe my wife is *selfless*. She models this
and has impacted my life and challenged me to do the same.

Here are a few pictures from over the years. Just where has this time gone?

Another benefit that I enjoy because of a wonderful wife is that I have no need for GPS or Google. The older we get and the more these minutes slip away, the more I enjoy her wisdom and knowledge. Ninety-nine percent of the time when we go somewhere, I drive. It's just how it's been with us.

But even though I'm in the driver's seat, don't think for a minute I'm the one completely in control of the car. She can turn on the windshield wipers, tell me the speed limit, let me know if there is a squirrel in the road, and has an uncanny ability to let me know exactly where I'm going and how to get there. I don't know how in the world she does it! I often say to myself (quietly until now), *"Who needs GPS, I have my wife."*

I think GPS actually stands for *"Gina's Personal Satellite."*

We had a good laugh when she pointed out this t-shirt to me on our twenty-eighth wedding anniversary trip. As we walked along the boardwalk in Ocean City, Maryland, she spotted this and said I should buy it.

I love my wife. Yes, she shakes her head and sometimes says, *"Whatever,"* but she is the best! I heard a comedian once say concerning husbands and marriage, *"Would you rather be right or would you rather be happy?"*

There is a guy in our congregation that says, *"Both."*

I hope my wife is laughing right now, if not, I'll probably be crying later.

Back in 1987, when we met, we did not know Christ. Neither of us grew up in a Christian home and had no clue about Jesus and His offer of forgiveness, grace, love, and mercy. We dated for a while, and then in April of 1988, I gave my life to Christ at a funeral home and a couple of weeks later, so did she during a Sunday night service at the altar of the Gospel Tabernacle Church in Arnold, Pennsylvania. Interestingly, that was where my Grandma had attended before she passed away, and that was where Gina and I would get baptized in water on Father's Day of 1988. And then on August 27, 1988, she became Mrs. Gina Mele.

Before we know it, we will celebrating thirty years of marriage. Actually, our daughter just married at the same age we were married, twenty-one, on October 14, 2016. Shortly after this, our son, Luke was married on July 7, 2017.

Just where has the time gone?

But the years between 1986-1988 changed our lives, our future, our destiny. In 1986, three of my grandparents died unexpectedly. Ten years later, my last grandparent passed away.

Joseph John Hollyoake: July 30, 1911 – April 23, 1986

Stella Hollyoake: April 27, 1917 – September 6, 1986

Harold Merle Mele, Sr.: October 10, 1914 – August 18, 1986

Verna Louise Mele: May 10, 1918 – September 16, 1996

The years that my grandparents were born and died are separated by a short little line known as a dash. If you take a look at every tombstone, you will find the year someone was born and the year they died, and in between, a tiny, little line. That "-" represents the years of our life. That little bit of time here on earth has such a major impact on where we will spend eternity and also what difference we are making here on earth in other people's lives as we're still living.

Unless Jesus Christ comes back, the odds of you or me dying are, one to one. That's 100 percent.

*"He has appeared to put away sin by the sacrifice of Himself.*

*And as it is appointed for men to die once, but after this the judgment,*

*so Christ was offered once to bear the sins of many. To those who eagerly wait for Him He will appear a second time, apart from sin, for salvation."*

—Hebrews 9:26b-28

I can't remember where, but I heard it said that *"the only thing you can take with you to heaven is a friend (or even an enemy)."* Why are we spending so much of our time here on earth building up our kingdoms when we could be spending it helping others to be there some day as well?

The wisest man, Solomon, realized this near the end of his life. Read his writings. Read them in this order, and you will see the different stages of his life.

He writes a beautiful love story when he was a young man called Song of Solomon.

In his middle years, he pens the majority of the Proverbs that give us so much wisdom today.

And nearing the end of his life, after the pain and struggles, the bumps and bruises that life brought his way, the Lord inspired him to write Ecclesiastes.

Look at these verses from the book of Ecclesiastes, my dad's favorite book of the Bible:

*"For I considered all this in my heart, so that I could declare it all: that the righteous and the wise and their works are in the hand of God. People know neither love nor hatred by anything they see before them.*

*All things come alike to all:*

*One event happens to the righteous and the wicked;*

*To the good, the clean, and the unclean;*

*To him who sacrifices and him who does not sacrifice.*

*As is the good, so is the sinner;*

*He who takes an oath as he who fears an oath.*

*This is an evil in all that is done under the sun: that one thing happens to all. Truly the hearts of the sons of men are full of evil; madness is in their hearts while they live, and after that they go to the dead.*

*But for him who is joined to all the living there is hope, for a living dog is better than a dead lion.*

*For the living know that they will die;*

*But the dead know nothing, And they have no more reward,*

*For the memory of them is forgotten.*

*Also their love, their hatred, and their envy have now perished;*

*Nevermore will they have a share in anything done under the sun."*

—Ecclesiastes 9:1-6

One day, before we know it, our toil on this earth will be over and *nevermore will they (we) have a share in anything done under the sun.* So, what are we doing with our little bit of time here on earth?

That short amount of time that we've been given? Are we living for Him, or simply for ourselves? Are we making our little "dash" matter? Are we making every beat of our heart and every minute of our days count? We're given only one shot at this thing called life, and it will be over before we know it.

As I said earlier, the great news is you are still alive because you are reading this book and you have been given another breathe.

I love how Jeremiah writes these words in Lamentations 3:22-23:
*"Through the LORD'S mercies we are not consumed, Because His compassions fail not.*
*They are new every morning; Great is Your faithfulness."*

Remember, old things have passed away . . . behold all things are new. If you have not been making your minutes matter, tomorrow is another day. It's not too late to get started. The Lord will show you, just as He continues to show me, the changes we must make to allow us to live our days to the fullest.

Let's keep reading Solomon's words in chapter 9 of Ecclesiastes:

*"Go, eat your bread with joy, And drink your wine with a merry heart; For God has already accepted your works.*

*Let your garments always be white, And let your head lack no oil.*

*Live joyfully with the wife whom you love all the days of your vain life which He has given you under the sun, all your days of vanity; for that is your portion in life, and in the labor which you perform under the sun.*

*Whatever your hand finds to do, do it with your might; for there is no work or device or knowledge or wisdom in the grave where you are going.*

*I returned and saw under the sun that–*

*The race is not to the swift,*

*Nor the battle to the strong,*

*Nor the bread to the wise,*

*Nor riches to men of understanding,*

*Nor favor to men of skill;*

*But the time and chance happen to them all.*

*For man also does not know his time:*

*Like fish taken in a cruel net,*

*Like birds caught in a snare,*

*So the sons of men are snared in an evil time,*

*When it falls suddenly upon them."* (verses 7-12)

Don't be ensnared in this evil time we are living in. My prayer is that the Holy Spirit is using the words in this book to get you thinking. To think about how you're using your minutes, your beats, and ultimately your life. I pray that it causes each of us to take a deep look inside our lives and grasp the reality of who we are, who Christ has called us to be, and how we need to look at our days as a *vapor* that is here and gone so quickly.

Isn't that what James is talking about when he writes (James 4:13-17):

*"Come now, you who say, 'Today or tomorrow we will go to such and such a city, spend a year there, buy and sell, and make a profit'; whereas you do not know what will happen tomorrow. For what is your life? It is even a vapor that appears for a little time and then vanishes away. Instead you ought to say, 'If the Lord wills, we shall live and do this or that.' But now you boast in your arrogance. All such boasting is evil. Therefore, to him who knows to do good and does not do it, to him it is sin."*

I believe James was reminded of the verses that David penned in Psalm 39:5-6 when he wrote the verses you just read,

*"Indeed, You have made my days as handbreadths, And my age is as nothing before You;*
*Certainly every man is at his best state a vapor.*
*Surely every man walks about like a shadow; Surely they busy themselves in vain; He heaps up riches, And does not know who will gather them."*

Notice that James points out that not only are the bad things we do called sin, but also the good things we're supposed to do, but choose not to do.

A saying that I will often use is "Lord willing." Why? Because that's what James reminds us to say here in God's Word, *"If the Lord wills . . . "*

Yes, we should plan and prepare for the future. As I write this and the year 2017 comes to a close, I'm already praying and planning for things coming up in 2018 . . . Lord willing. We must stop wasting our time on things that really don't matter and begin to invest our time in the things of eternity. We must stop procrastinating and putting off important things that need done today. Procrastination steals our time away as the enemy seeks to *"steal, kill, and destroy"* every one of our minutes.

I believe that one day we will answer for how we spent our time. Let's choose to spend our minutes wisely, not foolishly. Let's begin to pay our lives forward and make a difference with our days.

Take a look at those last few verses again from Ecclesiastes:
*"For man also does not know his time . . . "*
*" . . . the sons of men are snared in an evil time, when it falls suddenly upon them."*

The days we live in are evil. But let's not fool ourselves, they have been since Adam and Eve went hiding. It's so easy to get ensnared in the evil of our time if we're not careful. And if we do, the end of our time can suddenly fall upon us and our time here on earth will have expired. It would be great if, like a carton of milk, our lives had the expiration date already stamped on it. Or would it? But, if they did, how differently would we live out our days? If our expiration date were thirty days, six months, or even five years from today, how differently would we be living, loving, and forgiving those around us?

How much more would we laugh?

How much more would we give?

So, why don't we live this way if we know in all reality that our expiration date could be the very next minute? Would we make more of a difference and love others and share Jesus with more passion? Would we begin to do what I read on a sign at a church that said:

When it comes right down to it, life really is about the people we're blessed to have around us. Not things, not work, not hobbies, not retirement, not seeking self-fulfillment. It's about relationships. First and foremost with Jesus who died to save us and was raised to life so that we can have the Spirit that raised Him from the dead living in us! What a promise from His Word. Next to Jesus, this life then becomes about the relationships we have with others.

Something happened the night before my Grand-pap Joe died, the first of three that I lost in that tumultuous yet life-changing year of 1986. He was leaving our home in the evening and I was in my bedroom. As he walked past my window, I knocked to get his attention and wave goodbye. He never heard me and kept on walking without looking back. That night, he went home, laid down, and never woke up. Poof . . . he was gone.

Do you know how much I wish I could take that day back and run out that door and give my Pap a big ol' hug? Instead I sat lazily on my bed and just tried knocking on the window to wave goodbye. I would love to have given him one more hug.

Take time to call or be with the ones you love, and by all means forgive where forgiveness is needed. You'll have many regrets after they're gone if you don't.

To make every minute matter, we must grasp the meaning of laying down our lives for others. Here is a verse that you may be very familiar with:

> *"For God so loved the world that He gave His only begotten Son, that whoever believes in Him should not perish but have everlasting life."*
>
> —John 3:16

Probably the most popular verse quoted and memorized from the Bible. Great verse! But look at this verse from another of John's writings found in 1 John 3:16.

We must add this verse (and the ones to follow) if we are going to make every beat of our hearts matter.

> *"By this we know love, because He laid down His life for us. And we also ought to lay down our lives for the brethren."*
>
> —1 John 3:16

John 3:16 speaks about God's gift of eternal life, while 1 John 3:16 speaks of what we are to do with this wonderful gift of love that Christ poured out for us on the cross. The goal at the end of our lives is not only for us to get to heaven, but to invite others to go along as well. Jesus laid down His life for us, why? So that we can go to heaven. But there's so much more!

We must then be willing to lay down our lives for those around us. We truly can't live until we are sold out and ready to die. How do we do this?

> *"But whoever has this world's goods, and sees his brother in need, and shuts up his heart from him, how does the love of God abide in him?*

*My little children, let us not love in word or in tongue, but in deed
and in truth.*

*And by this we know that we are of the truth, and shall assure our
hearts before Him."*

—1 John 3:17-19

If we want to assure our hearts before God, we must begin to put
our faith into action. James, the half- brother of Jesus, puts it this way:
*"Thus also faith by itself, if it does not have works, is dead."*

—James 2:17

So let us begin to do the things today that will truly make a difference well beyond that ending year that will be on the right side of that
"dash" someday. To do so will always involve dying to self which is so
hard to do. That's why I believe the Apostle Paul said in 1 Corinthians
15:31, *"I die daily."*

We must learn to crucify our flesh, and until we learn how to do
this daily, we will never experience the joy and satisfaction of strength-
ening our spirit.

How can I sum this up? With my thoughts? No! Only His Word
has the power to change a life and to cause our beats and minutes to
matter. Only His Word has the power to set the captive free. Only His
Word can cut, shape, and mold us into who He wants us to be. Don't
neglect His Word, it's your very lifeline.

I end with these words from Ephesians 3:14-21 that sums up this
book in a minute.

This is my prayer for you.

*"For this reason I bow my knees to the Father of our Lord Jesus
Christ, from whom the whole family in heaven and earth is named,
that He would grant you, according to the riches of His glory, to
be strengthened with might through His Spirit in the inner man,
that Christ may dwell in your hearts through faith; that you, being
rooted and grounded in love, may be able to comprehend with all
the saints what is the width and length and depth and height – to*

*know the love of Christ which passes knowledge; that you may be filled with all the fullness of God. Now to Him who is able to do exceedingly abundantly above all that we ask or think, according to the power that works in us, to Him be glory in the church by Christ Jesus to all generations, forever and ever. Amen."*

CHAPTER 10 - SMALL GROUP DISCUSSION

If we all realize that we're going to die someday and our time on earth is so short compared to eternity, why is it that we can spend so much of our time building our kingdoms here on earth rather than in heaven?

- What does it look like to build your kingdom in heaven rather than here on earth?

If your life had an expiration date, would you live your days differently?

**Read James 4:13-17.**

- How differently should we be living when we keep these verses in mind?
- Are there people in your life that you need to forgive to begin living in freedom?
- What steps will you take to make this happen?

**Read 1 John 3:16-19.**

- Ask yourself, "Does my life line up with these verses?"
- If not, what changes could I make so that they come more in line with them?

# Conclusion

*"So teach us to number our days, That we may gain a heart of wisdom."*
—Psalm 90:12

DO YOU REMEMBER A TEACHER you had in school growing up? If you went to college, how about there? There are a few who come to mind immediately when I think of someone who taught me something. Dr. Carnahan was a professor of mine when I first entered college at Penn State's branch campus in New Kensington, Pennsylvania. One reason that I remember him is because he would not allow me to quit. College was all new to me, and his sociology class was very difficult for me just coming out of high school. After the first test, which I failed, I wanted to drop the class. I remember talking to Dr. Carnahan about it, and he would have nothing of it. He would not let me quit because maybe he thought if I quit at that, what more would I quit at in life. He challenged me to begin studying harder and give it a good effort. I believe that he saw something in me that I didn't see in myself. And so I persevered in that sociology class and ended up with a good grade, I believe a "B" for my 1984 fall semester at Penn State New Kensington.

There are many who taught me a variety of things about life. My mom and dad taught me so much growing up, thank you, I love you both. My wife and kids teach me many different things, and they probably don't even realize it most of the time. Friends and mentors of mine in ministry have taught me things over the years. I remember my first pastor and his wife, Pastor John and Sandy, teaching us about having a "family altar" time each day with our kids. To spend time reading some of God's Word, praying, and singing together as a family. My only other pastor, Paul Grabill, taught me to dream big and also keep things in perspective and not think too highly of yourself. He taught me things sometimes the hard way when he told me the truth. Ever have someone tell you the truth, and we all know that sometimes the truth really hurts, right? Sometimes the only way to grow is to hear the truth. It's how we respond to it that tells a lot about who we are. Some when they hear truth disagree with it and get angry and can even begin to be verbally combative. Others when the truth is told can swallow hard (which is sometimes difficult), take a deep breath and learn from it and grow. I believe this is part of gaining a heart of wisdom. If we are going to gain this "heart of wisdom," we must be willing to learn from our mistakes and weaknesses rather than get upset when someone shares truth with us. May we learn to respond with a heart of wisdom.

James gives us a clue of how to do this when he writes,
*"So then, my beloved brethren, let every man be swift to hear, slow to speak, slow to wrath;*
*for the wrath of man does not produce the righteousness of God."*
—James 1:19-20

When it comes to friends who speak the truth even when it hurts, remember this verse:
*"Faithful are the wounds of a friend, but the kisses of an enemy are deceitful."*
—Proverbs 27:6

It may seem like the ones who always tell us the things we want to hear and make us feel good are our friends, but they just may be at times our enemy. A true friend will sometimes look us straight in the eyes and say the hard things we need to hear to cause us to reflect inside of us and make us grow. Will it hurt? Sure, but that's why it says, *"faithful are the wounds of a friend."* A word of caution here. Don't always look for ways to correct someone with your words. Measure them carefully, speak them with gentleness, and allow the Holy Spirit to do the rest. Above all else, make sure all things are done with love because as Paul writes in 1 Corinthians 13:8, *"love never fails."*

Maintaining a teachable spirit is critical if we are going to grow and make every beat count. When someone responds to correction in a defensive manner or always points the finger at someone else, that person tends to never grow and mature into the person Christ wants them to be. May our hearts remain tender and open to correction because we can become blind to our own weaknesses. Find someone that you can receive honest answers from and be proactive and begin to ask them if they see anything in you that needs corrected.

A good one to begin with, if you are married, is your spouse.

I remember asking my wife a few years back, this question: *"Do you think I can be a prideful person?"*

Did I want to hear her answer?

Well, I had a feeling it was going to hurt, especially when she began with these words . . . *"Did you have to ask me that question?"*

She went on to be very honest with me. Hey, I asked for it, right? I don't know about you, but pride is something that can sneak up on us without noticing and begin to set roots in our heart if we aren't careful. I want to guard myself against pride because I know the Scripture teaches that *"pride goes before destruction"* (Proverbs 16:18). And the thing about pride is that most of the time others can see it in us way before we do, if we ever do. From time to time, I want to know how I'm doing in this area, and my wife is a good one to run things by. I thank her for telling me the truth and not just saying what I want to hear.

The Lord uses people to teach us things in life. There are people in each of our lives that play different roles and have a wide variety of personalities. There are certain people that all of us have that can speak into our lives and say things which can really help us make our minutes matter. Have you ever noticed how one person can say something and it not have much impact on our lives, but if that exact thing is said by someone who has influence over us, it can not only teach us something but possibly even change the entire direction of our lives?

As I come to the end of this book, I would like to share a little more about my friend, Evelyn, whom I spoke of earlier. She is eighty-eight years old. Each time I visit, I usually hear a different story from her, and it usually has to do with people that she has had the opportunity to influence in some way. The great thing about Evelyn is that I sense she doesn't even realize what an impact she has had on so many. Let's just say that I wish I could have been one of those kids that she took care of in her home and allowed them the experience of eating a fresh loaf of bread from the oven or simply coloring or making some craft at her kitchen table. And the stories I've heard over the last several years of visiting with her! I love to hear how simple life used to be and how much she enjoyed taking care of children in her home and also taking care of her family. Whether it be making meals, gardening, or making a beautiful quilt for someone she loved.

Why is it that we tend to look to famous people as ones who touch and change the world and really make their minutes matter?

Evelyn will never be famous in the world's eyes and believe it or not, she has never even flown in an airplane or driven a car. But the thing Evelyn has done so well is touch many lives. Some may underestimate the value of a woman who stays home to raise her kids, and even brings more into her home to care for during the day. Some may think that a mom who stays home with her children is wasting her talent. Mom, your children are young only once, don't miss the opportunity to imprint their hearts with your love and handprints. Whether you realize it or not, someone is going to and it might as well be you. You'll have plenty of time to work later, but you'll have only one shot at those kiddos. Evelyn has her handprints on so many lives and has instilled so many good values on the hearts of many.

May I ask, what is more important than that? Oh, the memories that so many have because of her. The stories, the warm bread straight from the oven, and even the times of correction to help shape and mold their lives. The playing in the yard, helping in the garden or the thirty-five plus quilts that she has sewn for her kids, grandkids, great grandkids and now even my daughter has one that she gave her for a wedding gift. Olivia is blessed to have one of these masterpieces. If only those quilts could talk.

No, she will never have her name on a sidewalk in Hollywood, but it will indelibly be imprinted on so many hearts. Evelyn simply made her minutes matter because she recognized the importance of people in her life and placed their needs before her own. Until we do that, we will never make our minutes matter. Evelyn lived out the golden rule that reminds us that *"whatever you want men to do to you, do also to them"* (Matthew 7:12).

Evelyn, thank you, for being you! Your stories have also impacted my life and for that I'm truly blessed. You have made your minutes matter, all 46,252,800 million (that's eighty-eight years' worth!) of them and they live on in the hearts and stories of so many.

Evelyn has taught me so much. She taught me about words. That what we say aren't just *words*, but they are *words that matter*. She taught me about time. It's not just the *hands on a clock*, but they are making our *minutes matter*. She taught me about the heart. That it's just not something that keeps us alive, but it's about making *every beat count*. Simply put, when it comes right down to it, we waste a lot of our time, so many of our heart beats on things that really don't matter in light of eternity. We can become very selfish with our time. But as we begin to live our minutes for something other than ourselves, then we begin to live! Maybe it's time to take a minute and reevaluate our priorities in life.

For truly, as Solomon said, everything does have it's time.

*"To everything there is a season,*

*A time for every purpose under heaven:*

*A time to be born,*

*And a time to die;*

*A time to plant,*

*And a time to pluck what is planted;*
*A time to kill,*
*And a time to heal;*
*A time to break down,*
*And a time to build up;*
*A time to weep,*
*And a time to laugh;*
*A time to mourn,*
*And a time to dance;*
*A time to cast away stones,*
*And a time to gather stones;*
*A time to embrace,*
*And a time to refrain from embracing;*
*A time to gain,*
*And a time to lose;*
*A time to keep,*
*And a time to throw away;*
*A time to tear,*
*And a time to sew;*
*A time to keep silence,*
*And a time to speak;*
*A time to love,*
*And a time to hate;*
*A time of war,*
*And a time of peace."*

—Ecclesiastes 3:1-8

So, what time is it for you, what time is it for me? I believe it's time to start making our minutes matter before they run out.

*Lord, thank You for each one who has picked up a copy of this book. I pray that the Scriptures You placed upon my heart to use as I wrote will touch and challenge each heart. May You give us hearts that strive to do Your work and Your will. May the beat of each heart line up beautifully with Your will. May we begin to see Your hand lead us more clearly in doing the things You say to do. May we not fear to go against the grain of this world. May we begin to, as it says in Scripture, view others and think of them more highly than ourselves. Help us to love and take time for the least of these. Help us all to truly make our minutes matter. Amen.*

# Endnotes

1. Walker, Jon, "God Controls the Timing in Our Lives," www.gracecreates.com.

2. "God never reveals his truth to a hurried soul." Quote by Chuck Swindoll.

3. Smith, Michael W., Song lyrics to "Breathe."

4. Sleep Foundation, www.sleepfoundation.org, "How much sleep do babies and kids need?"

5. *Wall Street Journal*; "How Americans Spend Their Time."

6. MSN Article, "30 Surprising Facts About How We Spend Our Time."

7. Bazin, Cynthia, February 4, 2016, www.success.com, "8 Things Successful People Never Waste Time Doing."

For more information about
## K.R. Mele
&
## *Minutes Matter*
please visit:

*www.rocknrollministries.com*

For more information about
AMBASSADOR INTERNATIONAL
please visit:

*www.ambassador-international.com*
*@AmbassadorIntl*
*www.facebook.com/AmbassadorIntl*